Teaching Values and Ethics in College

Michael J. Collins, *Editor*

NEW DIRECTIONS FOR TEACHING AND LEARNING
KENNETH E. EBLE and JOHN F. NOONAN, *Editors-in-Chief*

Number 13, March 1983

Paperback sourcebooks in
The Jossey-Bass Higher Education Series

Jossey-Bass Inc., Publishers
San Francisco • Washington • London

Michael J. Collins (Ed.).
Teaching Values and Ethics in College.
New Directions for Teaching and Learning, no. 13.
San Francisco: Jossey-Bass, 1983.

New Directions for Teaching and Learning Series
Kenneth E. Eble and John F. Noonan, *Editors-in-Chief*

New Directions for Teaching and Learning is published quarterly
by Jossey-Bass Inc., Publishers. Subscriptions, single-issue
orders, change of address notices, undelivered copies, and other
correspondence should be sent to *New Directions* Subscriptions,
Jossey-Bass Inc., Publishers, 433 California Street, San Francisco,
California 94104.

Editorial correspondence should be sent to the Editors-in-Chief,
Kenneth E. Eble or John F. Noonan, Center for Improving
Teaching Effectiveness, Virginia Commonwealth University,
Richmond, Virginia 23284.

Library of Congress Catalogue Card Number LC 82-84207
International Standard Serial Number ISSN 0271-0633
International Standard Book Number ISBN 87589-973-0

Cover art by Willi Baum
Manufactured in the United States of America

Ordering Information

378.014
T253

The paperback sourcebooks listed below are published quarterly and can be ordered either by subscription or as single copies.

Subscriptions cost $35.00 per year for institutions, agencies, and libraries. Individuals can subscribe at the special rate of $21.00 per year *if payment is by personal check.* (Note that the full rate of $35.00 applies if payment is by institutional check, even if the subscription is designated for an individual.) Standing orders are accepted.

Single copies are available at $7.95 when payment accompanies order, and *all single-copy orders under $25.00 must include payment.* (California, Washington, D.C., New Jersey, and New York residents please include appropriate sales tax.) For billed orders, cost per copy is $7.95 plus postage and handling. (Prices subject to change without notice.)

To ensure correct and prompt delivery, all orders must give either the *name of an individual* or an *official purchase order number.* Please submit your order as follows:

Subscriptions: specify series and subscription year.
Single Copies: specify sourcebook code and issue number (such as, TL8).

Mail orders for United States and Possessions, Latin America, Canada, Japan, Australia, and New Zealand to:
Jossey-Bass Inc., Publishers
433 California Street
San Francisco, California 94104

Mail orders for all other parts of the world to:
Jossey-Bass Limited
28 Banner Street
London EC1Y 8QE

New Directions for Teaching and Learning Series
Kenneth E. Eble and John F. Noonan, *Editors-in-Chief*

TL1   *Improving Teaching Styles,* Kenneth E. Eble
TL2   *Learning, Cognition, and College Teaching,* Wilbert J. McKeachie
TL3   *Fostering Critical Thinking,* Robert E. Young
TL4   *Learning About Teaching,* John F. Noonan
TL5   *The Administrator's Role in Effective Teaching,* Alan E. Guskin
TL6   *Liberal Learning and Careers,* Charles S. Green III, Richard G. Salem
TL7   *New Perspectives on Teaching and Learning,* Warren Bryan Martin
TL8   *Interdisciplinary Teaching,* Alvin M. White
TL9   *Expanding Learning Through New Communications Technologies,*
      Christopher K. Knapper
TL10 *Motivating Professors to Teach Effectively,* James L. Bess
TL11 *Practices that Improve Teaching Evaluation,* Grace French-Lazovik
TL12 *Teaching Writing in All Disciplines,* C. Williams Griffin

Contents

Editor's Notes

When Kenneth Eble, the editor-in-chief of this series, asked me to edit a sourcebook on values and teaching, I was happy to take the job. The topic seemed particularly important, and it had engaged my attention not just as a teacher, but as director of the values program in Fordham College and a member of the committee to restructure the undergraduate curriculum. I wanted to include chapters on the teaching of ethics, on the relationship of teaching to the social and intellectual setting in which it is carried out, and on what, in my experience, is the fundamental controversy about values and teaching—namely, whether one can explicitly raise questions of meaning, policy, and values in the classroom and at the same time remain consistent with the goals and methods of the discipline. My own teaching of literature in the values program told me one could do both, but I wanted others to face the question and discuss it from the perspectives of their own disciplines.

After a brief introduction, the sourcebook begins with an overview of values and teaching in American colleges and universities. Albert Howard Carter III surveys the various traditions through which values are consciously taught and then describes some of the ways they are communicated and affirmed implicitly. Mary M. FitzGerald, Catherine M. LaCugna, and Frederick J. Dillemuth discuss the relationship of values to the disciplines each one teaches. The questions they ask—Does literature teach values? Can theology be taught objectively? Is science a value-free endeavor?—are all, finally, concerned with the central tension between the claims of the particular discipline and the teaching of values.

In Chapter Six, Phyllis O'Callaghan describes a relatively new type of graduate program for adults, which affirms in its philosophy and format the ability of the various academic disciplines to illuminate and value individual lives and the world in which they are lived. Although Dr. O'Callaghan does not mention it, such graduate programs often attract teachers by providing them an opportunity to explore and make explicit the moral, ethical, and social implications of a given discipline.

The next three chapters are concerned with the teaching of ethics—or, as one of the writers would say, of moral philosophy. Carol J. Rizzuti, a teacher of philosophy, considers the question of who should teach ethics and how it should be taught. Ethics, she argues, is too important to be left to ethicians alone; if we say that ethical questions pervade all of life, then each discipline, in its own way, must make students aware of such questions. John M. Phelan discusses the teaching of ethics in a graduate program in communications. He distinguishes between students who plan to be working professionals and those who plan to be researchers, describes the world in which each group will work, and suggests how ethics should be taught to each group. Joseph Gerard Brennan describes the origin and development of a course in moral philosophy that he taught with Admiral James B. Stockdale at the Naval War College for senior military officers. At the same time, Brennan's chapter makes clear the consolation of philosophy for Admiral Stockdale during his nearly seven and a half years as a prisoner of war in North Vietnam. Although Phelan and Brennan teach students in specific careers, both reject the notion that, as Phelan puts it, "there is a special ethics for people in specific vocations."

In the final chapter, William R. Stott, Jr., affirms the teaching function of the university office of student affairs. Education should be concerned with the whole person, for students learn, develop, and grow, for better or worse, not just in the classroom and the library, but through the particular social and intellectual milieu in which they live and work and play. The volume concludes with some suggestions for additional reading.

I would like to thank some of the people who helped with this sourcebook. I am grateful, above all, to the nine contributors who recognized the importance of the topic and, despite many other demands on their time, generously agreed to write a chapter. Two people at Georgetown University were especially helpful: Dorothy Brown, associate professor of history and coordinator of academic planning, read and commented on an early version of my introductory chapter and Emma Harrington helped me put the manuscript in good order. Finally, I thank Kenneth Eble, not just for giving me the opportunity to edit this sourcebook, but also for his help and encouragement with the work.

Michael J. Collins
Editor

Michael J. Collins is dean of the School for Summer and Continuing Education at Georgetown University. He was formerly associate dean of Fordham College and director of its Values Program.

When college teachers fail to raise questions about meaning and values in their classes, they obscure the profound human significance of their disciplines.

Values and Teaching

Michael J. Collins

In a brief essay published in the *New York Daily News* on September 2, 1980, James N. Loughran, S.J., then dean of Fordham College, suggested some changes colleges must make if they are to transform freshmen "worried about jobs" into "men and women of intelligence, good sense, and compassion." What we need, he said, are "a college faculty rededicated to undergraduate teaching,... a more structured, coordinated course of study,... and a comprehensive vision," shaped by high schools and colleges, "of what they want to accomplish with the young men and women normally charged to them for eight years." As he explained in a subsequent essay (*New York Daily News,* April 21, 1981), his suggestions "raised an embarrassing question in two very different letters — one from a barely literate person, the other from a Fordham College alumnus of the 1950s: 'How is it that much of the evil in our world can be traced back to the activities and decisions of people with good college educations?'"

The question is a fair one, I think, and it cannot be dismissed simply by claiming that knowledge and virtue are unrelated, that the disciplines one studies in college have nothing to do with the conduct of human affairs. The claim, of course, is frequently made, if not explicitly, then at least implicitly in the way scholars generally carry out their research and teaching. The concern with method, the ideal of empirical objectivity, the pressure to specialize all conspire to obscure the relationship of the various academic disciplines to the world in which all of us must live.

M. J. Collins (Ed.). *Teaching Values and Ethics in College.* New Directions for Teaching and Learning, no. 13. San Francisco: Jossey-Bass, March 1983.

Philosophers analyze language and often ignore or declare irrelevant traditional questions of ethics and values. Literary critics examine the construction of a text and deny or disregard its referential power. Social scientists build paradigms and leave recommendations of policy to others. Historians narrow the focus of their research and produce specialized monographs that will be read only by other specialists. In an effort to be detached and scientific, scholars often seem to play games of chess among themselves and forget that their disciplines are originally and fundamentally our best attempts to know ourselves, our fellow human beings, and the world in which we live. Today scholars only rarely offer to write for the educated general reader, partly because they are not honored by their colleagues for doing so and partly because they have lost faith in their disciplines and believe their work has no relevance or value outside the closed system they themselves have created.

If the world at large is generally poorer as a result of such decisions, so, too, are the students who come to college these days. Anxious about the future, driven too often by the plans and expectations of their parents, they see college simply as the way to a good job or to a place in a prestigious professional school, not as an opportunity to make sense of their lives and discover what it means to live richly, wisely, and decently. More often than not, the courses they take — taught by scholars who value method, objectivity, and specialization — simply confirm this view of college and seem to be either irrelevant requirements to get out of the way or, at best, engaging intellectual games that have little to do with the lives they lead, day after day, in the dormitories across the street and in the town outside the gates. Students are too often cheated by their course of study, because so few of their teachers help them recognize that the disciplines they study, the courses they take, and the books they read are relevant to their own lives, that they raise and seek to answer such fundamental and abiding human questions as what is finally good and important and true. The questions are not academic; they must be answered at eighteen as well as at thirty-eight or fifty-eight, and even the best teaching and scholarship are finally trivial if they do not seek ultimately to make individual lives and the world in which they are lived richer and wiser.

College teachers, however, generally resist suggestions that the larger human questions, the moral and ethical implications of their disciplines, be made explicit in the classroom. For some, the resistance is epistemological: The discipline simply does not, as they see it, make any real reference to the world as it is. For others, the resistance is professional or pedagogical: The more explicit one makes these questions and implications, the more likely the objectivity, insights, and unique methodology of the discipline will be obscured, and it will become the point of departure for a freewheeling subjective discussion of "life."

Teachers of literature, to take one example, generally argue that the focus in the classroom must be on the text—on the unique properties of literary discourse, on *how* (not *what*) the text means. While this focus is initially justified, too often it gets no wider, and students never discover the power of a text to enlarge and illuminate their lives. If, as some would have it, teachers of literature discuss John Donne's vision of human love with a group of freshmen, who are no doubt falling in and out of love themselves, they may help the students gauge and understand their own experiences, but will fail to teach them literature, at least in the objective, analytical way in which it should be taught in an introductory course.

But such fears, I think, are finally groundless: one gets to the meaning of a text, to its distinct vision of things, only by knowing how to read it. Donne's vision of love is inextricably shaped by his way of expressing it, by the text in which it is embodied, by his use of metaphor, rhythm, rhyme, pattern—by his craft. The vision, the meaning, is had solely in the particulars of the poem, and we come to understand it in all its human richness and complexity only by apprehending fully the poem's formal richness and complexity. A focus on the text, the execution of method, alone leads to meaning, to insight, to the wider sympathy and understanding that literature brings. Donne the poet (not Donne the lover or Donne the thinker) gives his poems their profound human significance, and his exquisite poetic skill is in large part the reason why, as Helen Gardner (1962, p. 12) put it, "a whole generation in this century appropriated Donne and found in lines and phrases from his poems words that echoed the feelings of their own hearts." To work through a text is to work finally to a profound, complex vision of human life and of the world in which it is lived. If teachers of literature (or of any other discipline, for that matter) fail to make clear the human implications of what they teach, they not only narrow the significance of their own disciplines, but also deny their students one of the ways we all should have of understanding and making sense of things.

I once taught a course in drama that was paired with a course in the philosophy of Plato. The courses were open only to freshmen, and those who registered for one course had to register for the other. The courses were taught in Fordham College as part of its Values Program, and the teacher of philosophy and I were expected to use the material of each course to illuminate that of the other and then to raise explicitly, through the material, questions of meaning and values.

We began by suggesting that philosophers and playwrights both seek to reduce the chaos of experience—"the buzzing, booming confusion," as William James called it—to some kind of order and thus make it possible for us to understand our lives and the world in which we live. The teacher of philosophy recalled Graham Greene's statement (1971, p. 18) in his autobiography,

A Sort of Life: "And the motive for recording these scraps of the past? It is much the same motive that has made me a novelist: a desire to reduce the chaos of experience to some sort of order, and a hungry curiosity." I found another way of saying much the same thing in Northrop Frye's *The Educated Imagination* (1964, p. 64): "Our impressions of human life are picked up one by one, and remain for most of us loose and disorganized. But we constantly find in literature things that suddenly co-ordinate and bring into focus a great many such impressions."

The reading in philosophy began with *The Apology.* In it, Socrates restates two of the principles by which he has lived his life. He says, first, that what is true and just is true and just, no matter what the circumstances. Then he explains how one should live one's life: "Are you not ashamed," he asks his fellow Athenians, "that you give your attention to acquiring as much money as possible, and similarly to reputation and honor, and give no attention or thought to truth and understanding and the perfection of your souls?"

The play I chose to teach with *The Apology* was *The Glass Menagerie,* by Tennessee Williams. As I read it, the play asks Americans roughly the same question Socrates asked his fellow citizens more than two thousand years ago. Jim O'Connor, the "gentleman caller" of the play, wants, as he puts it, "success, money, and power." Tom Wingfield, the narrator, like countless American heroes before him, wants to escape, to join the Merchant Marine, because he is horrified by the prospect of spending the next forty years working for a firm called The Continental Shoemakers. Like *The Apology, The Glass Menagerie* affirms that we must do more than simply buy in — thoughtlessly and unreflectively — to the American (or Athenian) dream. "The unexamined life," says Socrates in *The Apology,* "is not worth living"; and the real failure of the Athenians to whom he speaks — and of Jim O'Connor, who is taking courses in public speaking and radio engineering to get ahead in a competitive, technological world — is that they do not examine their lives and ask themselves what is really important. For students who come to college, more often than not, to make the American dream come true in their own lives, the questions of how one examines one's life and of what is really important seem especially relevant.

Later in the philosophy course, the students read *The Gorgias.* The dialogue is about many things, but it begins with a discussion between Socrates and Gorgias of the right and wrong uses of rhetoric. Gorgias claims that once he has taught his students rhetoric, the art of persuasive speech, he has equipped them for success in the Athenian democracy and his work is finished. Socrates contends that one cannot simply teach rhetoric, but must also teach its proper use. For Socrates, the important thing is not the skill itself, but the way it is used, for good or evil.

The play I taught with *The Gorgias* was *The Birthday Party,* by Harold

Pinter. One of the characters in the play is a master rhetorician named Nat Goldberg, a man who uses language to dazzle and deceive everyone he meets. But Goldberg, it turns out, is hollow at the core. His words are only words: He has no beliefs, no values, no passions. He faithfully serves the system and sustains himself with right-sounding words that have no connection with reality. He is, to use Pinter's metaphor, propelled by hot air. Yet he is dangerous, for he uses language so skillfully, so surely, that he wins the admiration of the other characters and manages with words alone to destroy the one person who resists him. At a time when politics and theater are very often the same, when we are encouraged, by skillful words and even more skillful images, to buy a Ford or vote for Reagan, the questions raised by *The Birthday Party* and *The Gorgias* — how to use words and all our other skills, what to use them for, and how to defend ourselves against them — seem particularly important.

We linked other plays and dialogues throughout the semester, and the pairing of the courses was a great success for us and for the students. While the students learned, as they would in any course in drama, the distinct way in which plays give meaning, they also recognized the abiding significance of those meanings, particularly by their presence, more than two thousand years before, in the writings of Plato. More important, they came to understand the relevance of those meanings to their own lives and to realize that literature and philosophy could illuminate their own experience and help them to make sense of the things they were living through even as they took the courses. By pairing literature with philosophy, we were able to show the students the distinct method and character of each discipline and at the same time bring them to see how both disciplines seek to understand the same reality.

The pairing of courses in the Values Program was a success in another way as well, for it created, from what would ordinarily have been two distinct courses with different teachers and students, a genuine community. The teachers took great satisfaction working together — learning about each other's disciplines, sharing teaching strategies, sitting in on each other's classes, planning and taking part in the cocurricular activities the program encouraged (trips to the theater, panel discussions, debates), and especially working, for a change, with another person to make teaching and learning a cooperative undertaking. The students responded enthusiastically in the classroom and in their evaluations. They talked more both before and during the class, were more at ease with each other and their teachers, made friendships that lasted long after the semester was over, and generally felt that the pairing of courses had produced a humane environment in which teaching and learning could prosper.

Timothy S. Healy, S.J., the president of Georgetown University (1982, p. 233), recently offered some reasons why, in our technologically sophisticated world, universities "stubbornly teach poetry." Poets, he wrote, "like all

great artists. . . represent the 'points of intersection of time with the timeless.'"
They move in a "world of permanence" and their "voices. . . speak to all the
moments the young will face as they grow."

Georgetown is in the city of Washington, the capital of this enormously
rich and gifted nation, a beautiful city that draws countless visitors each year
and, despite three medical schools and one of the highest per capita incomes in
the country, has an infant mortality rate of 2.26 percent. The world the young
will live in as they grow is scarcely perfect, and the message from the city of
Washington these days is to get as much as you can as soon as you can because
you'll get no help if you don't. Colleges and those who teach in them can, if
they choose, close their gates on "the bent world," take the insular joys of
teaching, research, and writing, and in the process develop high-priced skills
in those who will simply "go with the drift of things" and settle into lucrative
careers. We cannot teach people to be virtuous. We cannot eradicate evil and
injustice with a liberal arts education. But when we develop in bright, talented
young men and women the skills to succeed in the marketplace, we give them
power, and we should, therefore, as Socrates recognized in *The Gorgias,* give
some attention to how they will use it — help them, through our teaching, to
become just, generous, and compassionate.

Our responsibilities to students are greater than we usually care to
acknowledge. We teach, individually, whether we want to or not, by example.
We teach by the way we run our dormitories, our athletic programs, and our
cocurricular activities. We teach by the way we conduct our classes and treat
our students. Above all, we teach our disciplines — and any discipline will, if
we let it, bring us sooner or later to the "world of permanence," to a confronta-
tion with meaning and values, to those fundamental and inescapable questions
that haunt every human life: Who are we? What is the nature of our world?
How are we to live? The questions, undoubtedly, will be answered, if only
implicitly, by the choices we make. If we ignore the questions as we teach, if
we leave them for students to discover or not as they will, then even our best
work is vain, for we will have failed in our most important and vital responsibility: to bring students to recognize that the disciplines we teach are finally
profound and serious ways not just to make sense of things, but also to help
them live rich, wise, and decent lives long after they have left our classes.

References

Frye, N. *The Educated Imagination.* Bloomington: Indiana University Press, 1964.
Gardner, H. (Ed.). *John Donne: A Collection of Critical Essays.* Englewood Cliffs, N.J.:
    Prentice-Hall, 1962.
Greene, G. *A Sort of Life.* New York: Simon & Schuster, 1971.
Healy, T. S. "From the University: Poets and Policymakers." *Washington Quarterly,* 1982,
    5 (1), 233–235.

Michael J. Collins is dean of the School for Summer and Continuing Education at Georgetown University. He was formerly associate dean of Fordham College and director of its Values Program.

In teaching values or morals, colleges and universities may use any of several explicit traditions. Perhaps even more powerful, however, are the implicit forces and forms that shape the values of professors and students.

The Teaching of Values in Colleges and Universities

Albert Howard Carter III

The teaching of values at the postsecondary level is currently a hot topic. The cannonical, "objective" education of the 1950s has given way, in many cases, to various kinds of relativistic discussion about values, and the renewal of general education in the 1970s has provided a curriculumwide format for the teaching of values at many institutions. This brief discussion cannot survey the 3,000 or so institutions of higher learning in this country, nor even all the formats and traditions of teaching values. Instead, it reviews some of the most common approaches to the explicit teaching of values, as well as some of the implicit, tacit, or even hidden ways in which values are taught. My thesis is that values are always being taught, regardless of a professor's avowed aims to be value-free. Educators, therefore, should be conscious of how values are presented, both in and out of the classroom.

Six Approaches to Teaching Values

Six traditions can be noted in the teaching of values (or morals; I shall use these words interchangeably). These are the inculcative, classical, experiential, growth-oriented, developmental, and preprofessional approaches. To be sure, these approaches may overlap in any given course. I have listed them

M. J. Collins (Ed.). *Teaching Values and Ethics in College.* New Directions for Teaching and Learning, no. 13. San Francisco: Jossey-Bass, March 1983.

in a rough order of historical predominance; thus, the inculcative tradition, while it can still be found, is largely out of fashion.

Inculcative. This approach assumes a specific set of values to be presented to and instilled in a student population. A libertarian outlook usually rejects this model as precluding informed choice; indeed, the Latin root of "inculcate," meaning "to stamp in with the heel," is hardly reassuring (see, for example, Kelly and Elmore, 1982). Public institutions, in particular, usually stay away from this approach, in part because of the doctrine of separation of church and state and in part because of a diverse student body. Private institutions have more choice, including relativist variations. For example, Berea College, as a private school, can announce the following aim for its general education program: "the capacity to make rational moral judgments based on an understanding of diverse ethical perspectives, including those of the Judaeo–Christian tradition." Thus, Berea College advances one set of values in the context of others. A different context would be that of professional or proprietary education, where a canon of ethics might be taught, such as Hippocratic and Pythagorean oaths at a medical school; again, the message would and should be tempered by other perspectives, including that of the individual student. Inculcative approaches, while easy to criticize, have the advantages of clarity and fidelity to a tradition that may be authoritative.

Classical. The typical ethics course is, perhaps, the common form of explicitly teaching values, either as a required course for all students or as a course available to philosophy majors and as an elective to outsiders. Typically, there is a survey of Western thinkers from Plato to Sartre, as in W. T. Jones and others (1962) or A. K. Bierman (1980). The approach is usually "objective" — that is, ideas are presented abstractly to students for their information. Classroom discussion may provide "real-life" examples of ethical situations, but exams and papers are oriented to content, not to application. The subfield of axiology, the study of values, would be a more technical form of teaching values. Axiology includes true-false schemata, decision diagrams, and universes where N truths might be possible. The advantages of this approach are theoretical rigor, historical depth, and an academic approach comfortable both to professors and students. Disadvantages can include ivory-tower abstraction, Western parochialism, and lack of connection with students' deepest concerns or pressing social issues.

Experiential. This approach comes from the American pragmatist tradition, particularly through Dewey, but it is as old as Plato's *Republic,* which specified that candidates for philosopher-king should be trained in specific active arts and skills that would develop the desired moral character for leadership. In the 1960s and 1970s, the demand for "relevance" meant, ideally, that academic knowledge should relate both to students and to the real world and help students analyze social issues, reach informed, ethical positions, and act in a socially responsible way. During these exciting (or dangerous, depending on your point of view) times, it was often students and young faculty members who used teach-ins, open-university courses, conferences, and experimental or pilot courses to show how practical-values inquiry might proceed. These formats, which led to such courses as The War in Indochina; Minority Rights; the Consumer and Business, all had the advantages of vividness, immediacy, and relatively clear implications for choices. Disadvantages included polarization into a narrow range of alternatives, hasty decisions, and the kind of commitment (even by the professor) that led to an inculcative approach within the experiential framework.

"Experience," of course, was usually at one remove, something like simulation or a case study approach. A course on the Holocaust or on ecology in industrial nations cannot repeat or stage the events to be studied, but it can present information and use vivid pedagogy such as films, eyewitness reports, and field trips to bring the events closer than a textbook can. Case studies in the classroom can help bridge *logos* and *praxis*; medical, law, and business schools frequently use case studies, not assuming a "right" answer, but saying, "This is the kind of thing you will encounter during your career." Experiential learning can occur outside the classroom, of course, with or without values exploration. When values are studied, though, the result can be powerful; Outward Bound, international travel, and internships in business or social services are a few examples.

Growth-Oriented. These approaches gained great popularity in the late 1960s and early 1970s, a second wave of innovation after the experiential, "relevant" courses. Roots include the works of C. G. Jung, third-force psychology, Carl Rogers, the Esalen Institute, the growth movement in general, and Sidney Simon (1972, 1975) in particular. One of the most visible and pervasive traditions, this approach touched many high schools, colleges, and universities throughout the 1970s; it is now on the wane, as the developmental and preprofessional approaches expand. In some ways, the growth-oriented approach to the teaching of values was a personalized version of the experiential approaches, bringing values questions not just to the individual student but also to his or her immediate world; values clarification dealt with the individual's use of drugs, attitudes about sex, and handling of money or time. The advantages of this approach were immediacy, focus on the individual, relevance, and utility. Possible disadvantages included a lack of historical or social breadth, lack of intellectual rigor, and a kind of gimmickry that conservative professors found trendy, frivolous, or simply misguided. In the late 1970s, values education emerged from two new bases—the theoretical base of developmentalism and the practical base of job training (hence, preprofessional courses).

Developmental. The bases for this approach are in the work of Piaget

(1965 [1932]), Kohlberg (1958, 1971), and Perry (1970). In some cases, the developmental course could be called informational, because the values education is not intended to change students' values but, rather, to inform them of a particular developmental scheme. In other cases, theory per se is less important, and the course does, indeed, intend to promote moral development: John M. Whiteley's Sierra Project at the University of California–Irvine used a course, "Moral Development and Just Communities," as well as a dorm setting (Whiteley and Associates, 1982). One of the questions for continuing research is the impact during one semester of Piagetian or neo-Piagetian models on late adolescents, not to mention their impact on returning college adults of all ages. Another theoretical problem is the interplay between abstraction and behavior: College courses are good at theory, but values development occurs most often through real-life stimuli and reinforcements. Thus, the retreat from the growth-oriented courses may, by default, allow the campus environment, for better or for worse, more power in shaping students' values. It is my impression that developmental courses, despite the rigor of theoretical backing, are not nearly so pervasive as the growth-oriented courses were.

Preprofessional. These courses have spread more quickly than the developmental courses did. They are typically not offered through general education, but through a major—for example, ethics and journalism, biomedical issues, fair business practices, legal ethics, and so on. Their general aim is to acquaint students with values issues and decisions within particular professional fields, thus providing a transition from the academic world to the world of work. In format, they vary from a regular, full-credit course to a one-credit course, perhaps in combination with an internship or some in-house application of professional skills. An example of the latter arrangement would be the graduate course required of beginning teaching assistants. Even if such a course is not labeled as values-oriented, the values issues are numerous—fair grading, plagiarism, responsibility to students with different levels of preparation, and the general question of good service to a clientele. When preprofessional courses are offered to majors only, the benefits are obviously limited to those students, and values teaching becomes subdivided by specialty.

These six approaches to the teaching of values suggest a wide range and variety of concepts, subjects, and formats. Clearly, faculty members, both as teachers and as curriculum planners, have maintained a strong interest in values education; over the last four decades we have seen not only many kinds of values education but also relatively rapid evolution of courses. Values education has responded to the intellectual currents of the day, changing more quickly than other sectors of the academic world. (By comparison, the response of higher education to the computer revolution seems slow.) The turmoil in values teaching reflects a search for the "best ways," a search that is not over. I anticipate new combinations of the six approaches sketched above, as well as the development of new approaches. Alverno College, for example, is pursuing a "total learning environment" approach that includes courses, residential affairs, and career services, all working on eight competencies throughout the institution in a four-year program. One of the competencies is valuing and decision making: Students progress through various pedagogical levels by contracts and assessment, not by course requirements. Alverno's approach includes most of the approaches discussed here (but not, in any strict sense, the inculcative) (Earley, Mentkowski, and Schafer, 1980).

There is much potential, and there are interest and growth on many fronts. There are also change and evolution, however, including something of a retreat from relevant and growth-oriented courses. Also, there are some changes in the intellectual climate that are not favorable to explicit values education.

Implicit, Tacit, and Hidden Approaches to Values Teaching

Regardless of approach, aim, philosophy, or format, the academic world is always teaching values, even when it claims to be objective or value-free. Here are two illustrations.

The "Aging Hippie" Professor. In this case, a 1970s-style professor is at odds with the institutional norms, which appear to be evolving toward 1950s models. Professor X still values a personal-growth orientation, close contact with students, a high degree of self-disclosure, "relevant" courses dealing with current social issues, and a pedagogy that relies more on process and exploration than on content or authority. The institution, however, is moving toward more "professional" education, preparing students for jobs; it emphasizes content, facts, skills, data bases, authority, information transfer, and highly sequenced curricula with little flexibility. Perhaps Professor X is tolerated as a token guru, a permissible aberration; perhaps he or she is tenured and not easily eliminated. Perhaps Professor X will leave the institution and even the profession. We must observe that it is not just Professor X who represents values; the institution itself has a strong, if unexplicit, set of values, too. Indeed, the institution's tacit values are immensely powerful, owing partly to their safety from public discussion, their tacit incumbency within an administration that is always watching the "bottom line," and a coalition of professors just emerging from graduate school in these "professional" times with those educated in the 1950s and now taking power through administrative roles.

The Committed, "Professional" Professor. Here we have a scientist, Professor Y — a traditional, conservative professional who, in the course of his or her research, has become involved with ecological concerns. He or she has served on planning and assessment boards in the community, but has not found a place in the curriculum to present the values issues he or she increasingly finds to be most important. Thus, the professional growth of Professor Y is not readily interpreted to students because of implicit values buried in institutional structures, rules, and procedures.

Perhaps these two illustrations can help us realize how heavily value-laden institutions are, whether or not they are aware of such positions. Thus, "the medium is the message" in academia as well as in mass communications. By its very format, an educational institution is a purveyor of values, a collection of values claims: "It is worth your time and money to study with us"; "We can supply you transferable and salable skills"; "Our requirements are good for you"; "We do it better, more cheaply, and more prestigiously than anyone else." Such claims are rarely stated, tested, or evaluated, however, largely because faculty members and administrators tend to debate mechanical details (budgets, credit hours, evaluation procedures, curricular adjustments) *ad nauseum,* without touching on the larger and most basic values questions of higher education. A campus milieu comes, by default, to be one of the most powerful teachers of values, while values courses (if any exist) are relegated to one portion of the curriculum, especially if they are courses limited by pedagogy (to be, say, largely information) or by subject (offered in only one pre-professional area). Values education becomes situational, a sociological happenstance well out of control of the institution; and the strongest teachers may include drugs, plagiarism, "jockismo," "getting by," cutthroat competition, anomie, fraternities and sororities, and so on. There are colleges and universities, particularly smaller ones, that are making conscious efforts to shape the total educational environment, but my impression is that academics are more commonly moving away from the teaching of explicit values within a community orientation. While cause and effect are hard to discern, there are two polarities in American higher education that profoundly influence the teaching of values, both in its explicit and implicit forms.

***Hard* vs. *Soft*.** This polarity has many faces: science *vs.* humanities (Snow's "two cultures"), quantitative *vs.* qualitative, serious *vs.* frivolous, objective *vs.* subjective, absolutist *vs.* relativist, data-based *vs.* anecdotal, and so on. (Mildred Henry and Joseph Katz (unpublished) discern "Z" *vs.* "J" types in Omnibus Personality Inventory profiles.) In each of these pairs, the first word tends currently to be the more prestigious and authoritative and to represent the approach more likely to be funded by administration, by government, and (through enrollment) by students. This tendency toward implicit values of "hardness" has had a dulling effect on the explicit teaching of values, which is often regarded as a luxury or even a delusion, since the "hard" tradition tends to assume fairly absolute values and proceeds, with little reflection, to act on them, while the "soft" tradition seems never to produce any answers (certainly not statistical ones), only never-ending commentary. The "hard *vs.* soft" polarity of style, epistemology, and pedagogy has reinforcement from still another polarity of institutional purposes, discussed below.

Job Training vs. *Liberal Arts.* This dichotomy offers both a grave threat and an interesting challenge to higher education. It is not entirely new, of course, but the new vocationalism of the past half-dozen years is so powerful, and institutions have been in such precarious positions, that sweeping changes have come about in only a few years on campuses across the nation to train students for jobs through courses in business, management, accounting, and computer science. Fully equipped with external validating agencies (and the sometimes questionable authorization of the business community), the job-training movement has institutionalized its values pervasively, often at the expense of liberal arts values, including wide-ranging studies, curriculum flexibility, deferred career choice, and foreign language and travel. The greatest pity is that these two thrusts should have become adversaries at all, since a combination of them would be immensely attractive, useful, and valuable. What typically happens, however, is that the implicit teaching of values through job training supplants the explicit teaching of values through the liberal arts.

Both polarities are destructive of the best efforts of students, professors, and institutions; and they exist, unhappily, because of the academic community's lack of self-scrutiny. Self-study documents can generate hundreds of pages on floor space and other mechanics, but little on the place of values in an institution. To vary the ancient dicta: "Institution, know thyself!" Or, "The unexamined institution may not be worth attending." The dangerous, divisive polarities we have reviewed here can be healed, so that the strengths of each pole are still available, but not in opposition to the other. This healing could come through discussion within an institution; administrative and/or faculty leadership; in-service professional development of the faculty, the administrators, and the staff; and a general urge toward institutional synergy. The poles should supplement, not combat, each other; Professor X and Professor Y should respect, support, and complement each other.

I believe that values education works best when the following three conditions are present: (1) an approach (or a combination of approaches) that has been reached consciously and reflectively — one that strikes students as vivid (this may include affective, spiritual, and even primal appeals), important ("relevant"), and intellectually sound; (2) a reinforcement of classroom experience by such dialectics with the "real world" as field trips, campus-life programs, career counseling, and the study of the human body as in a high-level wellness approach (Ardell, 1979); and (3) an institutionwide awareness that makes implicit values explicit, debated, and modified, if necessary, into a common vision that students, parents, alumni, and the immediate community as well as faculty and administrators can understand.

Values education has taken many forms and will doubtless assume many more. I believe that (1) institutions will best teach values through conscious discussion, imagination, and cooperation (even among polar opposites); (2) institutions should select from among intellectual models and fashions, but should never forget the interests and needs of students nor "real world" connections; and (3) in general, institutions should keep explicit values explicit and make implicit values also explicit.

References

Ardell, D. B. *High-Level Wellness: An Alternative to Doctors, Drugs, and Disease.* (Rev. ed.) New York: Bantam, 1979.

Bierman, A. K. *Life and Morals: An Introduction to Ethics.* New York: Harcourt Brace Jovanovich, 1980.

Earley, M., Mentkowski, M., and Schafer, J. *Valuing at Alverno: The Valuing Process in Liberal Education.* Milwaukee, Wisc.: Alverno Productions, 1980.

Henry, M., and Katz, J. *Turning Professors into Teachers.* Unpublished work.

Jones, W. T., Sontag, F., Beckner, M. O., and Fogelin, R. J. *Approaches to Ethics.* New York: McGraw-Hill, 1962.

Kelly, K. E., and Elmore, M. J. "Guarding the Hearts and Minds of Students Against the Threat from the Right," *Chronicle of Higher Education,* 1982, *23* (14), 5.

Kohlberg, L. "The Development of Modes of Moral Thinking and Choice in the Years Ten to Sixteen." Unpublished doctoral dissertation, The University of Chicago, 1958.

Kohlberg, L. "Stages of Moral Development as a Basis for Moral Education." In C. M. Beck, B. S. Critenden, and E. V. Sullivan (Eds.), *Moral Education.* New York: Newman Press, 1971.

Perry, W. G., Jr. *Forms of Intellectual and Ethical Development in the College Years: A Scheme.* New York: Holt, Rinehart and Winston, 1970.

Piaget, J. *Moral Judgment of the Child.* New York: Free Press, 1965. (Originally published in 1932.)

Simon, S., and Clark, J. *Beginning Values Clarification: Strategies for the Classroom.* San Diego: Pennant Press, 1975.

Simon, S., Howe, L. W., and Kerschenbaum, H. *Values Clarification: A Handbook of Practical Strategies for Teachers and Students.* New York: Hart, 1972.

Whiteley, J. M., and Associates. *Character Development in College Students.* Vol. 1. Schenectady, N.Y.: Character Research Press, 1982.

Albert Howard Carter III, is associate dean of faculty for general education and professor of comparative literature and humanities at Eckerd College, St. Petersburg, Florida. Some of the information for this chapter was gathered at an Association of American Colleges workshop on general education and faculty development held in Washington, D.C., June 4–6, 1982.

The study of literature moves students through stages of growth in intellectual appreciation and in analytical ability, each stage bringing with it values that enhance those already assimilated.

Values and the Teaching of Literature

Mary M. FitzGerald

The most perplexing questions—the perennial questions—are usually the most satisfying ones to debate. The question of whether or not literature teaches values is one such question; and, although it has been puzzled over by literary critics and by writers of poems, plays, and fiction, it has not been resolved yet and continues to be a subject of contention in the classroom. Certainly it is for my students, and certainly it was for me when I sat on their side of the lectern some years ago, arguing against one of my wilier professors in a hot, springtime classroom that the teaching of literature and the teaching of values were completely incompatible.

The Argument for Value-Free Literature

Literature, I explained to him passionately, was its own justification, its own law. By its very nature it was not didactic: The study of literary works did not teach ethical lessons; values were extraneous and irrelevant to art. Whatever views others might hold, I said pointedly, this was the view held—and held correctly—in my discipline (his field was history; mine was literature). To say otherwise, that values could be taught through literary study, would be to reduce art to propaganda, a notion so intellectually revolting that

M. J. Collins (Ed.). *Teaching Values and Ethics in College.* New Directions for Teaching and Learning, no. 13. San Francisco: Jossey-Bass, March 1983.

any clear-headed analyst would be forced virtually to favor the opposite view — that propaganda was a perversion of the literary impulse, and that literature should not — and, properly understood, does not intend to — teach. To force values into it, or to force them from it, would be to impose the knowledge of good and evil on a world that did not have such knowledge and did not need it.

For examples of how badly literature fared when values were deduced from it, one had only to look at Marxist critics celebrating the class struggle in a work, at the expense of the artistry, or at any religious or irreligious orthodoxy censoring and distorting a writer's meaning. When values were grafted onto it, literature was just as badly served: For example, there was Rudyard Kipling humbly acknowledging Victorian England's dutiful sovereignty over "lesser breeds without law." Like all art, literature could be seen to be free, by virtue of its intrinsic nature as the expression of an individual consciousness, which itself ought to be utterly free. Instead of looking for values in it, or using it to justify a particular course of action, one should take it solely on its own terms, whether as a single literary text or as a whole body of work. The greatest writers invariably did just that, and so did the best literary critics.

How, then, might one judge "good" literature from "bad"? Perhaps there was neither good nor bad, but only literature. How, then, could there be greater and lesser writers? Well, one made judgments, after all, but these were based on criteria inherent in the nature of literature, not derived from external standards. One studied meaning; one evaluated the fidelity of the work to the individual and universal experience of mankind; one examined inner harmonies and looked for consistencies of structure, content, imagery, and tone. What resulted from such study was an appreciation that was both intellectual and emotional. What if a particular work was lacking in one or more of these elements of perfection? Then it might be said to be unsuccessful, to some degree, but this judgment was valid only in terms of literary values, not in terms of extraneous criteria.

The history professor let me have my say; the ironies were, perhaps, so self-evident that no argument was needed. If literature was as utterly free as its writers were, then its freedom was qualified, at best. Moreover, as an activity of men and women, it might very well be seen to reflect their values, which would presumably be either in harmony with the values of their respective societies or in reaction to them. Worst of all, I had talked myself into a corner — his corner — by invoking absolutes like "fidelity," "harmony," "consistency," and a standard of perfection against which failings might be judged. If literary study could be said to teach these abstract qualities, then it implied a value system that might well have validity in the real world as well. Learning how to judge literature might possibly teach analogous lessons about living.

We never learned the professor's actual view on the subject, as he played the devil's advocate on this as on all other questions raised for our edification. To have made his opinion clear would have spared us from having to work it out for ourselves. All the same, I doubt that he agreed with my argument, and I suspect he was pleased to see me trapped in my own logical web. There was something in his look that suggested I would someday know better than I did then.

Twelve years on his side of the lectern have given me a different opinion, although they have not completely reversed my view. I still believe that literature is not directly concerned with shaping moral consciousness; that writers legitimately can explore even morally reprehensible ideas with impunity, because by doing so they name and conquer the fears that beset our condition — much as Adam, in naming the beasts in the Garden of Eden, signified his hegemony; and that art is art *because* it is not life. The arguments were not new when I made them, and they have not changed much since then, but I know now (I may even have suspected it then) that the study of literature teaches values, whether we want it to or not.

Nothing could be more obvious to a classroom teacher, and it is surely good to admit it and try to understand how it comes to be so. We are fooling ourselves if we think that there is such a thing as "pure" literature or "pure" science; we may envision the possibility of such an abstraction, but the abstraction originates in "the fury and the mire of human veins," as Yeats would say, and its echoes continue to be felt along the pulse. Literature teaches values not only because it reflects (at least to some degree) the values of the writers who produce it, but also because it is an act of communication and, as such, necessarily involves an intention to communicate meaning — even if the intended audience is small or merely a later version of the writer, and even if the intended meaning is no more ambitious than asserting that a certain arrangement of letters can make a noteworthy sound or shape.

The issue is, admittedly, even more complex. An outside system of values applied to a text teaches more about the system than about the text, and a value system formulated in studying a work of literature is so intimately entangled in the work as to be almost inapplicable to real life — almost, but not quite. Practically speaking, as we see it in the classroom, literature does not exist purely to teach lessons or ideas, but it does not and cannot exist completely apart from them. The truth of the matter (as with all perennial questions) lies, paradoxically, at both extremes or, perhaps, hovers between them. In taking our students into a literary text, we inevitably set them in search of absolutes like perfection and truth and beauty, values in an artistic context and values in life. The study of literature moves students through stages of growth in intellectual appreciation and in analytical ability, each stage bringing with it values that enhance those already assimilated.

Stages of Growth in Students' Valuing

No student arrives before us utterly without values or utterly without ability to handle a literary text. Despite that fact (or, perhaps, because of it), teachers usually face some initial difficulty in conveying the literal meaning of a text. This task is harder than it sounds, particularly in the United States in recent years, where television is geared to a sixth-grade vocabulary and where, consequently, students and teachers alike can be disheartened by the students' need to fumble constantly through a dictionary, as well as by the absence of the traditional common body of human knowledge: A freshman in a state university can write of "Atom and Eve," for example, and an entire sophomore seminar in an Ivy League college will never have heard of Job. My own rude awakening to this fact of life came when three successive classes missed a line from Keats's famous sonnet on Chapman's Homer, about lands "which bards in fealty to Apollo hold." The first class had no idea of what "fealty" was (the dictionary had not helped). The second had never heard of Apollo (he was not in the dictionary). The third mistook bards for anything but what they were (they had not checked the dictionary). More recently, a student looked up "Homer" and produced a reading centering on the travels of a pigeon heading for the Pacific. All these examples underscore the need to inculcate a certain set of values: the discipline and integrity necessary to settle for nothing less than strict accuracy and letter-perfect comprehension.

This goal passes quickly from being an end in itself to becoming the means by which students encounter a larger issue—the degree to which the reader's freedom to interpret a text is limited by the writer's actual words. Whether students are aware of the process or not, they are discovering values in the act of searching out the simplest, most inclusive interpretation of a given set of words. They are balancing internal freedom against external control, and they are having to be consistently open-minded, learning to be wary of preconceptions and receptive to the ideas of others. These attitudes will develop as students progress in literary study and will also be applicable to the world beyond books.

Having learned to think openly, students must relearn how to think critically, this time from a literary perspective. For some reason, in recent years the question of personal interpretation against the demands of the actual wording of a text has proved to be a problem especially fraught with struggle. Most students arriving in college literature classes have not had much experience as disciplined readers; therefore, almost the first critical judgments they make are value judgments on the content of a work. They will approve or disapprove of a writer's point, and they will argue forcefully for their right to see the text in their own way. It takes very careful and continued explanation that opinion is *not* interpretation to save the teacher from the charge of imposing a single viewpoint on the students. (New instructors invariably find students making this complaint on teacher-evaluation forms.) It takes time for students to accept the principle that any interpretation not contradicting the writer's words and not adding more than is there is permissible. There follows an understanding that some readings will be better than others, and that the best readings are both full and uncomplicated. What this process teaches, apart from the literal meaning of the texts being read, is the need to be self-critical, analytical, and aware — in short, to hear what is actually said and to see reality as separate from merely personal views.

Getting to this stage is the necessary prelude to deeper understanding, and it is often surprising that even the better-prepared students will not be able to produce more than a merely mechanical application of the literary terminology and other critical paraphernalia we sometimes too eagerly teach novice readers. Students need to be able to submit to the words on the page without allegorizing, decoding, or interpreting them beyond their simplest meanings. When they can do this, they are ready to evaluate the content of a literary work on its own terms, rather than as a reflection of their own personal experiences. At this level of reading, they expand their environment through the vicarious experience of fictional personalities and events. Obviously, this is the point where they are likely to find themselves learning values especially applicable to real-life situations. To the extent that the subject matter of a literary work deals with moral choices, students will inevitably be made to confront those choices, if only to determine the literary effectiveness of the work. They are exposed to a range of occurrences larger than that to which they would normally have access, and, inevitably, their own value systems are challenged, confirmed, or altered in the process. Especially when contemporary material is involved, this can make for an electrifying — even painful — class, particularly when ethnic, religious, or cultural presuppositions close to the root of a student's self-image are challenged by those of a writer (and, implicitly, by the wider reading public, which has determined that this writer's work is to be studied).

To say that literature does not teach values is not to have taught such an electrifying, painful class. Reading William Faulkner with black students or taking white students into James Baldwin's territory, for example, can demonstrate very quickly how values are defined, tested, and sharpened against a literary text. Even when a class discussion is not especially heated, the teacher can be aware from watching silent students that some sort of growth or change is taking place within them. When cultural values are adopted or discarded, it can seem like a rite of passage or like a catharsis. By inhabiting someone else's world — even a fictional one — students can radically revise received systems of values, becoming more clearly defined as individuals in the process.

In less extreme circumstances, where the perceptions at stake are less intrinsic to the identities of the students, the expansion of personal awareness may seem less extensive, but, in subtler ways, it is no less so. A young person trying to evaluate the emotions of King Lear, or someone with no direct experience of death trying to understand the old mother in Synge's *Riders to the Sea,* who has lost her husband and all her sons, is stretching his imagination to encompass emotions beyond those he already knows, which he must do before he can determine how effectively the writer has presented the character. This effort means growing into the experiences of another life and developing values in terms beyond merely personal references. What this development teaches is obvious — respect for other people and other cultures, not only abstractly but also concretely; the student will see real-life individuals differently as a result. In this respect, the study of literature is the study of humanity.

Higher Levels of Understanding

Teaching students to live through literature in this vicarious way, however, is not really our primary purpose. This level of understanding is an initial phase in a complex analytical process, which involves a more aloof, critical appreciation. Students cannot evaluate a writer's choice of diction, structure, or incident until they fully comprehend, emotionally and intellectually, the ideas or situations the author intends to convey. Once they have done this, they proceed to the next, more literary, critical level. This is nothing less than the search for perfection: It takes the given text and the ideas presented in it, imagines what a perfect expression of the writer's intended meaning would have had to be, and examines the extent to which this particular manifestation of the idea lives up to that standard of excellence. To do this properly, of course, students need to be familiar not only with the range of characters and incidents the author had available, but also with the literary forms and techniques, together with examples of those forms and techniques at their finest.

The values taught in this literary-critical exercise are primarily aesthetic: The students learn to take delight in an author's fidelity to the truth of experience (whether real, imagined, or fantastic), in the power of imagination, in the appropriate choice of words and structures to convey particular meanings, and in a harmonious proportion of the parts to the whole. They are learning the importance of attempting the absolute best in the production of any fine thing. The values learned, challenged, or strengthened in this phase of study have ramifications well beyond aesthetics: the value to society of aesthetically trained human beings is great in itself. And, for the individual student, there is enormous satisfaction in finally being able to say, in an informed way, that a certain poem, play, or novel is the best of its kind or fails to meet its potential. The more students read, the more they study what is really being

said, and the more they evaluate the manner in which it is said, the more satisfaction they inevitably feel. If they are becoming writers themselves, then they
are not only growing in their understanding of the creative process, but are
also learning to control and impose order on their world.

Once students have reached this level of interpretive ability, they are
likely to apprehend literature as a discipline in itself, different from the study
of science or of philosophy. Protracted study in other fields, however, gradually will bring them around to the realization that these are only different
aspects of the same unified reality. Here, though, is where they are likely to
assert that literature exists in and for itself, that its rules inhere in its nature,
and that it is meant to be contemplated for its own sake. Here, again, the
values imparted are those of aesthetics (wholeness, order, harmony) and of
practical life (the play between freedom and control, between what the artist
wills and what the material will allow). They will read the critics, encountering
varying points of view that will not only challenge their understanding of specific texts, but will also teach them that the discipline of literature may itself be
understood from a variety of perspectives. Openness to a full spectrum of
critical ideologies may suggest that literature is more clearly perceived through
some critical approaches rather than through others, and that it is illuminated,
at least in part, by all. (The example I use is fairly ordinary—a mountain
perceived in the varying light of day.) If they decide to choose a particular
methodology of their own, they will do so—if they are honest with themselves
and not swayed by the teacher's preference—only after a rigorous evaluation
of all critical approaches, and thus employ their system of personal and artistic values in yet another capacity, reinforcing the sense of informed open-
mindedness as well as honing logical skills.

Great Literature's Concern with Values

Mastery of this sense of literature as a whole and familiarity with the
major texts and major critical methodologies are usually all we ask of our
undergraduate majors in literature. At the graduate level, however, and occa-
sionally earlier, they will be asked to engage in the intensive study of a relatively small area of literature, so as to become intimately familiar with the
work of a single writer or perhaps of a small group of writers. At this point in
their careers, students will confront the central value position in much
teaching of literature: Only those writers who have confronted the great questions of life repay the trouble of reading. Whatever their felicity of phrasing,
whatever the richness of their imagery, whatever the number of their works,
those writers who have not come to terms with suffering, death, and all the
sorrows and joys of living will seem hollow or incomplete. They simply do not
hold our attention for long periods of time. Without the sense of an evolving

personal philosophy of life, no writer is a great writer; and so, ultimately, the study of literature is involved with the study of values, in this deepest sense.

If a writer comes to envision a purpose or a meaning in life, which he is able to express in an arresting and appropriate way, then his work impels study and rewards it. When we talk about works that have "stood the test of time," we are attesting to the validity of this principle; there is not only beauty in what they write, but also a view of life relevant to our own experience, regardless of our circumstances. Such writers have penetrated to a level of universal truths about the human condition, and it is worth the effort to become so familiar with their works that their words stay in our minds when the books are closed and can be continually invoked and evaluated against our own experience. For me, this relentless pursuit of another's writing has meant, recently, following William Butler Yeats along some labyrinthine paths. For others, this pursuit is primarily a study of Shakespeare, Dante, Donne, or Beckett. One does not stop with the work of one great writer; one starts there and moves through others, gradually refining concepts of form, style, or metaphorical system, but also judging the adequacy of response to the larger issues that have always affected humankind.

Inevitably, then, literature teaches values. Colleges insist that students have a minimum exposure to literary texts, not merely to enhance students' ability to express themselves, but also because the study of literature is a discipline in itself—and because there is a continuing belief that exposure to the life experiences of real and imagined others can impart something of value. Students experience this exposure in various ways, depending on their level of critical sophistication, and that experience is subject to growth and change. Writers at their work may not intend this experience directly; they are more immediately concerned with expressing their ideas in the most perfect manner possible. But confronting experience at the most profound levels of intelligence, and the determination to convey it memorably and well, are echoes of the divine "I am"—an assertion that existence is valuable in itself, an answer to the perennial question of whether life is worth living with Molly Bloom's immortal "Yes." If we can teach this to our students, then we will have taught them well.

Suggestions for Reading

The question of the practical worth of literature has been debated in literary history since the time of Plato, and I am indebted to a very large range of critical writing. Any standard textbook in literary criticism will supply a bountiful reading list for future pursuit of the topic. A very fine recent discussion is found in Gerald Graff's *Literature Against Itself: Literary Ideas in Modern Society* (Chicago: University of Chicago Press, 1979).

Mary M. FitzGerald is an associate professor of English at the University of New Orleans. Her specialty is Anglo-Irish literature, and she has written recently on Lady Augusta Gregory and the poet Richard Murphy.

Can theology be taught objectively? What are the
epistemological issues entailed in this question?

Theology, Epistemology, and Values

Catherine M. LaCugna

When Nietzsche's madman announced in the nineteenth century that God is dead, that the Creator-God had bled to death under our knife, surely theology might have been expected to be transformed. But Nietzsche's slogan merely encapsulated changes already taking place in the history of ideas. Nihilism did not appear from nowhere, nor, as we shall see, were theology and the teaching of theology left unaffected by the murder of God.

Is not the death of God a strange starting point for a chapter on the possibilities of teaching theology today? I think not. Nietzsche's anguished cry signals an earlier time, when God was being unlatched in other ways from the world (and so, presumably, left to die in God's remote heaven). Immanuel Kant had already posed the bold question of whether reason was capable of grasping the noumena believed to be behind phenomena or was confined to knowing only phenomena, and these only as they appeared to be—filtered, as it were, through the foreordained structures of human consciousness. Kantian skepticism (or agnosticism), which introduced the distinction between "pure" and "practical" reason, effectively relegated all classical epistemological claims about reality to the realm of pure reason. For Kant, there are no means of knowing the existence of the objects of pure thought (such as God) except in an a priori way—but this way is impossible; empirical knowledge alone (practical

M. J. Collins (Ed.). *Teaching Values and Ethics in College.* New Directions for
Teaching and Learning, no. 13. San Francisco: Jossey-Bass, March 1983.

reason) is able to make judgments of truth. Therefore, nonempirical criteria for theological claims simply are not forthcoming; the existence of God (if there is one) cannot be affirmed by reason unless God is accessible to empirical measurement, which, by definition, is impossible.

There was a precedent for Kant's critical question in the view of Descartes, whose "methodic doubt" resulted in the construction of scientific method as we know it today. The Cartesian *cogito,* with its turn toward the knowing subject, meant that now all truth and meaning resided not with the transcendent God, but with the knowing self. Mathematics became for Descartes the ideal model for seeking truth, for there the estrangement between subject and object, knower and known, was nearly total.

From Descartes and Kant, the history of reason took only a few steps to reach Ludwig Feuerbach, who formulated one of the most devastating and lasting critiques of religion. For Feuerbach, theology is anthropology — that is to say, a statement about God is nothing more than a statement about humanity. Feuerbach argued rather forcefully that God is a projection (note the psychological term) of human consciousness thinking itself to be absolute. Theology, then, is an enterprise whose object is God only in the sense that we are God or that consciousness itself is divine.

Descartes, Kant, Feuerbach, and Nietzsche are only four of the critical thinkers belonging to the fascinating intellectual history from the Enlightenment to the present. They are mentioned here because they, perhaps more than others, made decisive philosophical moves that, in the long run, threatened not only the object of theology (God), but also its very status as one intellectual discipline among others. As a result of their and others' contributions, our modern *intellectus* can be characterized by its skepticism, which throws into doubt all transcendental types of knowledge; by its secularity, which makes all legitimate knowledge immanent; by its scientism, which exalts scientific method as noetically normative; by its relativity, according to which all knowledge is relative to the knower and to the knower's spatio-temporal-social location; and by its subjectivity, which shifts the authority for knowledge from outside to within.

Are these conditions in which theology can survive? Even if we believe so, must theology imitate other academic disciplines and strive for an objectivity prescribed by academics whose methods are shaped largely by Cartesian and Kantian views of knowledge and values? Can theological pedagogy be required to detach itself from the material the teacher seeks to convey? These questions raise what I take to be the central difficulty in teaching theology today — the tension between academic demands for an objective, scientific approach to the subject of religion and the peculiar characteristics of theology itself, which call for a transformation of the very same conception of objectivity. It is my contention that objective (or value-free) theology is a contradiction in terms, both for general epistemological reasons and specifically theological ones. To argue this point as a theologian, however, I will first need to set out some general observations on the epistemological issues at stake.

Objectivity as a Goal of Knowledge

Thesis Number 1. Value-free interpretation, in any field, is an illusion. Perhaps we are justified in using Freud's meaning of "illusion" (a wish seeking fulfillment) to ask whether value-free interpretation, or so-called objectivity, was not the greatest illusion produced by the early users of scientific method. Fortunately, today this thesis hardly requires defense, except on the level of the most popular (and frequently distorted) understanding of science, where people have not caught up with theoretical developments in the contemporary philosophy of science. It is generally agreed by both humanistic scholars and "pure" scientists that scientific method (hypothesis–experimentation–verification) is as value-laden as any other intellectual activity. Method itself is never entirely separable from either the user of the method or the matter under investigation, but classical scientific method urged the investigator to "bracket" his or her biases, presuppositions, expectations, and beliefs and adopt an attitude of indifference, disengagement, and detachment.

During the 1920s, in theoretical physics, Werner Heisenberg's formulation of the uncertainty principle threatened this scientific belief system, and not long thereafter the advent of Einsteinian physics seemed to complete the dismantling of classical science. Yet the popularized version of science persists, according to which it is believed that science can do or prove anything, provided that scientists are given adequate budgets and sufficient time for research. Popular consciousness goes along, unenlightened, with its persistent demand for proof and verification, despite the fact that exceedingly little about our world can be proved, even in the strictest scientific sense. Least of all can scientific method itself be scientifically verified.

In theology, efforts were made to imitate scientific method, although with uneven and sometimes damaging results. In the eighteenth century, Schleiermacher revolutionized theology and theological method by claiming that the starting point for reflection is the self's experience of God. He singled out the feeling of absolute dependence as the one element common to all religions and, thus, the only defensible place to begin studying theology. Theologians still argue today about whether or not this Cartesian turn to the subject vitiates theology, because the subjectivist principle, it is said, is methodologically atheist (Murray, 1964). A second example of theology emulating science is the emergence of what is called systematic theology, which attempts to organize in a clear, consistent, coherent, and organic fashion all the various doctrines and other elements of theology in their historical and confessional contexts. One could very well ask whether this is at all possible, given the nature of theology and the unpredictable, nonsystematic human element in the religious experience that engenders theology. Furthermore, theologians today are preoccupied with questions of methodology, and although these questions are important, it is tempting to become engaged in theoretical issues and never go beyond prolegomenal considerations. We certainly may dispute whether or not the scientific model is a good one for theology, but the same involvement–detachment question raised in science must then also be raised in theology.

Bias in Theology

There is a great deal of discussion today about hermeneutics and methods of interpretation. When a scholar deals with a text, presumably he or she strives to let the text speak for itself, that is, to avoid exegesis, reading extraneous elements into the text. In the nineteenth century especially, following advances in philology and historiography, biblical theologians began to investigate the Old and New Testaments in a literary-historical-critical fashion modeled after the scientific notion of neutrality. Those methods were believed to prevent scholars from imposing their intellectual or confessional biases on a text, but this ideal, too, proved impossible: Modern historiography carries with it a number of assumptions drawn from a particular world view, and contemporary feminist and liberation hermeneutics have shown how presuppositions can exercise political or partisan functions (Schüssler Fiorenza, 1982). Theological interpretation, then, cannot suppose itself to be free, on hermeneutical grounds, of bias or hidden agenda.

One of the biases theologians once sought to "leave outside the laboratory door" was their faith. Because, in the eighteenth and nineteenth centuries, rationalism supervened on religious beliefs of any kind, theologians who emulated their scientific contemporaries believed that the perspective of faith added onto a text or an event something that was not there in the first place. No doubt, faith in God is a perspective through which one sees things in a certain way. But there is a second half to this truth: Having no faith in God is in equal measure a perspective through which one sees a text or an event. In other words, atheism and agnosticism are as biased as theism is, for each position entails certain assumptions and conclusions about the nature of reality and about our varying ability (or inability) to grasp reality's meaning and value. Theologians felt embarrassed by their faith in God and thought their only choice was to detach themselves from their religious traditions. Misled and confused, theologians became philosophers of religion, whose task was to debate the intelligibility of theological claims according to certain rational criteria. Others became phenomenologists and historians of religion, whose task was to describe (never to evaluate) religious claims. But in prescinding from their faith, these thinkers traded in the one thing that would have rescued their work from the descriptive and empirical and qualified their thinking as genuinely theological.

A second matter that has come to some prominence in science is relativity. Although Einstein used the term in a technical way to refer to the relationship between location, gravity, and the passage of time, almost immediately his principle was translated into its crude popular form: "Everything is relative." The imprecision of this slogan detracts from its point — namely, that all truth claims can be reduced to mere opinions, which are to be "measured" by their location in intellectual time and space. The theological equivalent of Einstein's popularized principle pertains to religious pluralism, to the fact that not only are there many world religions with competing world views, there are different views of the same event even within one religion. In the question of how to impart this knowledge, it is often expected that a professor can or will remain detached from the subject matter in order to avoid judgments thought to be inappropriate or impossible. But this is to assume (erroneously, I think) that all views of truth are equally acceptable or equally valid and that there exist no metacriteria by which we can adjudicate various world views. Again, if objectivity is defined differently from the way it is used in science, then relativity, as it is usually understood, must likewise be re-evaluated.

The Positive Function of Bias in Theology

Thesis Number Two. Value-free or detached theology is a contradiction in terms because of the nature of theology. Theology is, strictly speaking, discourse about God or about God's relationship to men and women. Often theology is construed to be the same as the philosophy of religion or the philosophy of God, but there is this decisive difference: Theologians submit to the prior authority of revelation, which is defined as God's self-communication. Revelation is the datum which particularizes theology, and theologians proceed from revelation to the startling claim that we can speak about God, even though there is much disagreement about the extent to which this is possible. The principle holds just the same: Theologians believe it is their task to speak about God, even while they recognize the paradox that makes it ultimately impossible to do so. On this basis, theological epistemology and pedagogy can be expected to raise fresh problems and assume unique features.

Objectivity in Theology

All disciplines are characterized by what Aristotelian philosophy conveniently calls their "formal objects" — in the case of theology, God, or God in relation to us. It is axiomatic that a method must be designed and allowed to emerge in a way that suits its formal object. Thus, literary criticism cannot be empirical in the way that biology is; theology cannot be immanent in the way that historiography can. Since the object of theology is unlike any other, theological method must be tailored to fit it—if and insofar as this is possible. Without plunging into the discussion now being conducted about theological method, I shall offer one pertinent illustration.

Torrance (1969) has suggested that the objectivity of theological knowledge consists in an application opposite to the usual scientific sense of the term: Theological knowledge cannot be detached and indifferent, but must be devoted to and bound up with its object; therein lies its rationality. Theologians are obligated to "so submit ourselves to the dictates of the object that we think in terms of it, and not in terms of what we think we already know about it" (p. 35). In this effort to preserve the a priori nature of revelation, Torrance differentiates between detachment from presuppositions and detachment from the object. Detachment from suppositions is what scientists and theologians alike strive to achieve. Detachment from the object is simply impossible—and undesirable—in theology.

Whether or not one agrees with Torrance's view, theological epistemology cannot be expected to conform to the noetic and rational criteria produced by other fields of discourse, whose formal objects are quite different. At the same time, however, one cannot wish theology to claim exemption from general standards of rational discourse, rigorous thinking, and communication of results.

The Nature of Theology

Theology, then, is rational discourse about both God and God's relationship to the world. As one would expect, theologians scrutinize religion or religious consciousness. Religion may be defined as the response of an individual or a communalized set of responses to a powerful word or event that is transformative for the hearer of the word, the witness of the event, or the recipient of a tradition. Since religious response is precisely the focus of theological study, we cannot expect theologians to remain detached in the laboratory sense from religious response. Certainly, individual theologians may not have identical experiences, but it can be assumed that they are sympathetic to the fact of religious experience and are convinced, at least generally, that it is true.

One can conduct what is called the "scientific study of religion," through which the scholar seeks out universal or particularized symbols, myths, or typologies as they function within a certain religious tradition. But this endeavor is not the same as theology, precisely because theology is not an indifferent intellectual activity. When the scholar is moved from the study of religious responses per se to reflect on the nature of the word or the event eliciting the response and, finally, to reach judgments about both the nature of the event and which responses are warranted and how they should be understood, then the religious scholar becomes a theologian.

Theology as Confessionally Rooted. Judgments about who God is or is not and how we are to understand experiences of God are theological, not phenomenological, judgments. Yet even though the theologian, in making such claims, does so with certain value convictions in mind; theological judgments also have a confessional dimension. Whether one is a Lutheran, a Roman Catholic, or another kind of theologian, one tries to ask and answer the questions that a concrete community finds itself unsettled by. Roman Catholic theologians are far more likely to ask questions about forms of ministry (male or female; ordained or nonordained; celibate or noncelibate) than their Methodist counterparts are. One of the paradoxes of theology is that it is rooted in a concrete, believing community, apart from which it retains no function or authority. This is not to imply that theologians are "party line" adherents, whose only role is to justify the claims of the group, for theologians also exercise a critical function with respect to their communities. Still, this function always requires adherence to the group's fundamental truth claims. Value-free or detached theology in this arena is clearly a contradiction in terms.

Teaching Theology. When one is asked to teach theology in an academic setting, especially at the college or university level, the thorny question arises about the values implied in doing so. If theology, as a form of knowledge and as a kind of activity, functions in the ways described here, then teaching theology will always entail the holding of values on both epistemological and credal grounds. Serious misunderstandings generally arise on the second of these grounds: Is the task of theology to convert? What is the teacher's relationship to his or her students? Is the task of the teacher to convert, to convey information, both, or neither? Perhaps these options set up false heuristic limits; true learning, after all, is much more like conversion than like the passive reception of data.

The equivocal use of "conversion," with its religious and pedagogical overtones, may serve only to confuse in this discussion. But the metaphor holds fast, and we ought not to shy away from its use. Aquinas' famous dictum, "Love is the lamp of knowledge," summarizes the insight that learning (about the self, others, the world) takes place as one "puts on the mind of" or is "impinged upon by" the subject of study. Truth—if one believes it is even partially accessible and graspable—must be independent of intellectual construction and distortion; in other words, it must be allowed to emerge and speak for itself. "Conversion" is an exact term that denotes the "turn towards": towards the other, away from the self, towards what is to be known and loved, away from the machinations and deceptions of the self. Professors (as university teachers like to be called) choose their profession presumably because they have some vision of truth to profess. Whether or not they admit it, even those who pretend to be vision- or value-free are advocating a certain (mostly negative or agnostic) view of truth.

Theologians, no less than other professors, entertain convictions about reality and our relative ability (or inability) to discover truths about it. But are theologians trying to convert, in the usual religious sense of proselytizing? Here, perhaps, confessional differences would account for different answers, and perhaps a seminary is different from a university. As one who teaches theology in a university, I would answer that it is not the theologian's responsibility to convert doctrinally, nor (even if it were possible) to produce or simulate religious experiences for students, but, at best, to act as any professor in any field must act — to seek to remove intellectual misunderstandings of and obstacles to the visions we find compelling. Most basic for me is the conviction that reality can be known because God is its origin, ground, and goal. Obviously, this idea cannot be conveyed easily, nor to every student, but this difficulty is surely no indictment either of theology or of its vision.

Theology as Academic Study. I am opposed to religious indoctrination. The counterbalance to a pedagogy that would reduce theology in this way can be derived, I think, from the usual academic setting of theology. As in any other field of inquiry, certain professional standards of intellectual honesty, responsibility in research, respect for students' freedom, and commitment to rigor should prevail. Academic theology is not exempt from, nor need students of theology fear the outcome of, rigorous intellectual challenges to the truth claims based in the faith perspective. With skillful guidance, students in theology courses should come to appreciate theology as one legitimate form of inquiry among others, an enterprise seeking by its methods to discover truths about the nature of God, about God's relation to us, and about ourselves. Only those who have not examined their post-Enlightenment epistemological prejudices would maintain either that theology has no place in the academic world or that theology cannot meet the highest intellectual standards.

Summary

The question of values in teaching is an epistemological one: Can we know what is true? Can we know what is good? Theologians are inclined to maintain that we are at least relatively or partially able to know and discern meaning and value, because meaning and value are waiting to be known and discerned. If holding this conviction is what is meant by being biased, then let us gladly forsake "objectivity" and joyfully and purposefully embrace this "bias." If, among biases, our two basic choices are between thinking that we cannot really know things as they are in themselves and thinking that we can know (however we qualify this thought), then the second choice of bias seems infinitely preferable (although utterly complex), far more enticing because it is risky, and rather well suited to the happy task of intellectual (not religious) conversion through teaching.

Nietzsche's madman gleefully proclaimed the death of the God who, before dying a thousand metaphysical deaths, had taken the soul from humanity. Today, with equal confidence, we can announce the death of the god of objectivity, which, by protesting its detachment too loudly, has taken the soul from the quest for truth. Theology is by no means opposed to science or objectivity; on the contrary (and this fact is frequently overlooked) theology and science work hand in hand, as each seeks to ascertain truth by its own proper methods. No inquiry is ever conducted, no truth is ever attained without at least a conviction that the undertaking is worth the intellectual struggle.

References

Murray, J. C. *The Problem of God.* New Haven: Yale University Press, 1964.

Schüssler Fiorenza, E. "Feminist Theology and New Testament Interpretation." *Journal for the Study of the Old Testament,* 1982, *22,* 32–46.

Torrance, T. F. *Theological Science.* New York: Oxford University Press, 1969.

Catherine M. LaCugna is assistant professor of systematic theology at the University of Notre Dame. She is the author of
The Theological Methodology of Hans Küng *(Scholars Press, 1982).*

Science itself may or may not be ethically neutral,
but its study and pursuit are not value-free.

Values and Ethics in Science

Frederick J. Dillemuth

Science Is Ethically Neutral

Let me begin with a simple proposition, unproved yet widely held: Science is neither a blessing nor a curse; ethically it is neutral. Ambivalence adheres to science tenaciously; but what human endeavor is not characterized by ambivalence? Indeed, one might question whether or not ambivalence is inherent in nature itself. The element nitrogen, to cite but one instance, is rightly called both the preserver and destroyer of life, since it is essential for the production of both protein and explosives; and the example of atomic energy is too trite and too hackneyed to bear repetition here. As Leonard K. Nash (1962) so aptly writes, "Conceivably there is some knowledge that can lead only to 'evil'; certainly there is none that can only lead to 'good'" (p. 90).

One could go on at length in this vein, but let us not belabor the point. The fact that one admits that science in itself is neutral or is marked by ambivalence (although not necessarily in application or in practice) is not *ipso facto* to question science's worth on the grounds that its study and pursuit are value-free. To be sure, science does not perforce instill an ethic as dramatically, immediately, or thoroughly as does an immersion in the thoughts of Aristotle, Aquinas, or Kant. But one might question whether any course of instruction, no matter how conceived or executed, teaches values or an ethic. Rather, we might argue that people acquire ethics or internalize values by being exposed to or following the examples of other people, real or fictional.

M. J. Collins (Ed.). *Teaching Values and Ethics in College.* New Directions for
Teaching and Learning, no. 13. San Francisco: Jossey-Bass, March 1983.

I am not naive; I advance no extravagant claim that the study of the natural sciences—physics, chemistry, or biology, for example—or even the history of science itself will alone make a person more moral, honest, or civilized. Over the course of centuries, humanity has shown precious little self-restraint. We never have, and we never will teach people to be virtuous. The best we can do—and this is a great deal—is to expose them to disciplines in which ethical values are highly prized. Cecil Schneer (1960) is probably correct when he writes, "The realm of morals, of values, of ethics—of all that can be considered under the heading of purpose—is out of the reach of science, although science is not out of its reach" (p. 12). Many people, with a frightening regularity and a glibness that reveals their lack of depth, repeat this sentiment, as if the study of science—or, better yet, its practitioners—have nothing to do with morals or with ethics. In a very true but possibly somewhat circumscribed sense, the scientific endeavor would be practically impossible without these values.

What does the ordinary citizen expect of any dedicated scholar and of natural scientists in particular? Among other things, it might be scrupulous dedication to objectivity. This does not imply that professional scientists frequently yield to the temptation to deceive; far from it. Research workers in the sciences often enough have no particular vested interest in the results of their experiments. But scientists, no less than other people, are shaped and influenced by the milieu in which they live, the spirit of their age. This influence is carried willy-nilly into the laboratory or library carrel. It is the task of dedicated scholars to cast off the often invisible and unsuspected fetters that hamper investigation and prevent them from following unsuspected and fruitful paths of research.

Objectivity is no less elusive for physical scientists than for poets. Indeed, for scientists a lack of objectivity is all the more pernicious, since it is neither warranted nor expected. It would be intriguing to speculate where we would be now in astronomy if there had not been a persistent (and, possibly, basically unfounded) preoccupation with the circle until the seventeenth century. Would the "ultra-violet catastrophe" have caused such consternation or have existed at all had physicists been able to question the "common sense" but unwarranted supposition that energy can be absorbed or emitted continuously rather than in discrete quanta? Possibly, too, willingness to question ingrained convictions of a nonrotating earth and a geocentric universe might have prevented untold embarrassment for both Catholic and Protestant divines.

Is There an Ethical Content to Science?

In the course of over twenty years of teaching chemistry, I have been asked—sometimes obliquely and sometimes directly—"Is there an ethical content to science? Should teachers and students expect that values can even be found, much less taught, in the study of fields other than the humanities?" In one sense, the question is specious: One does not study mathematics, for example, in order to lead a more moral life; sociology, theology, and ethics are more appropriate fields for moral development. To expect that a knowledge of statistical thermodynamics will of itself guarantee moral behavior is to expect delivery of something the discipline was never intended to provide. I do believe, however, that studying the natural sciences imparts, as a by-product, a good number of necessary or at least useful values. These include lack of prejudice, dedication to truth, perseverance, willingness to abandon previously held positions, ruthless honesty, accuracy, deep and abiding appreciation of the rationality of nature, and a disposition to admit ignorance, something bordering on humility.

One pernicious tendency we poor humans must combat incessantly is our proneness to prejudice. I do not speak primarily of this evil in its more overt forms, though it is not inconceivable that scientific progress has at times been hampered, that breakthroughs have been ignored, because the discoverer was of the wrong race, the wrong nationality, the wrong religion, or the wrong sex. One could ask whether all of the early opposition to the theory of relativity could have been attributed to scientific difficulties alone. This gross form of prejudice, which never should have found a place in science, is, I feel, quite rare at the present time. However, as Albert Camus writes in *The Plague,* the virus is never wholly dead, it has a tenacious hold on life, it can exist as spores, ready to break out into activity at a moment's notice. I refer to a subtle prejudice, however, to an attitude of mind that forecloses openness to the unexpected, the new and possibly unsettling.

Among the many adages culled from the writings of the Romans is this phrase: *"Veritas tametsi caela cadant":* "Truth, even though the heavens should fall." Quite often, scholars prefer (subconsciously, in the main) that the heavens remain unshaken, rather than that truth appear in all its troubling novelty. Recall the opposition aroused by Semmelweis when he proposed that puerperal fever was due to blood poisoning, rather than to pollution from the atmosphere. Certainly, in the beginning if not later, the glimmer of truth, the faintly suspected reality, is upsetting. Old paradigms must be abandoned or at least drastically altered. Neat solutions to which men and women have grown accustomed suddenly become less satisfying, as new data challenge their validity. The community and the scientist himself experience discomfort, landmarks grow less prominent, certainty wavers: The old, the tried, the eminently satisfying is no longer so.

At this juncture, the ruthlessly honest scholar must be able to withhold judgment, reject commonly held tenets, and admit the possibility that all is not well with the theory and that no amount of well-intentioned tinkering will restore the discredited mechanism to its pristine glory. This is not easy to do. Everyone, not only the much-maligned college student, seeks closure, feels distraught in the face of ignorance, and secretly wants a definitive answer to the question "What do the authorities say?" And if there are no "authorities"? It is precisely at such a watershed that unblinking honesty must be the order of the day. Most investigators are honest, but all of us are loathe to jettison deeply cherished ideas. All of us tend to view reality through our own mental constructs. While not precisely failing to see the forest for the trees, we still make ourselves blithely ignorant of telltale facts that point ever so subtly to a hidden and more comprehensive reality. Perhaps this ability to make the leap, to see significance in things that others ignore is more rare than we have imagined. How simple for Kepler to have brushed aside a discrepancy of eight minutes of arc in the orbit of Mars as due to quite miniscule and acceptable experimental error in the observations of his preceptor, Tycho Brahe.

It has been claimed that we live in the age of the cheap, the shoddy, and the make-do, of appliances that break down with frustrating regularity and of "durable goods" that are so in name alone. In the scientific community, however, publication of sloppy or even deliberately spurious data meets with severe condemnation. Nothing is said in secret; rather, findings are proclaimed from the housetops. Extravagant claims, results that cannot be verified, and experiments that cannot be repeated are certain roads to loss of credibility and respect. Thus, science is an excellent mode of instilling the values (virtues, if you will) of accuracy, painstaking effort, and pride in achievement.

In his book *The Road of Science and The Way to God,* Jaki (1978, p. 311) writes, "Science in part owes its existence to the courage of men and women in raising questions regardless of the difficulty of getting proper answers." I would carry the argument one step further: The steady advance of learning can be ascribed to the adamantine wills of people who persist in asking questions in the face of the very real possibility that there are no answers at all. It is not skepticism to say that some enigmas may never be completely resolved, despite our most diligent and careful efforts.

Matter, apparently, is ineluctably opposed to mind; at least some Scholastic philosophers would have it so. Perhaps too, by an ingenious twist of the uncertainty principle of Heisenberg and by reflection on our own thought processes, we can become aware that it is impossible ever to characterize completely the material universe, much less control it. Almost automatically, in our attempts to reduce reality to a coherent system we make assumptions and analyses that rely heavily on causality and continuity, concepts valuable in the macroscopic world, but questionable or, rather, undemonstrable on the lower, more basic levels of reality. Assuredly, cosmic speculation such as this does not affect the everyday progress of science, yet in those rare and quiet moments when the mind is free to range over the entire realm of reality, realizing that some problems may never be resolved is a humbling experience. The courage to face this possibility unflinchingly and go on undaunted is a value greatly to be admired. This trait of man was starkly outlined by Homer, who in his *Iliad* wrote, "The Gods have cursed thee with a mind that cannot yield."

The Study of Science Is Not Antiseptic

The human spirit embarks on no endeavor without fear and trepidation, and the more momentous the undertaking, the greater the terror. Few fields of learning yield such variety and excellence of practical and theoretical results as the natural sciences do. This affirmation is no doubt open to cavil and dispute; be that as it may, the study of science is not, nor need it be, a value-free, antiseptic endeavor. Imperceptibly yet indelibly, it molds the character of the devotee with thirst for knowledge, courage in the face of failure, ruthless honesty, and willingness to learn, advance, examine new discoveries, and abandon cherished but outmoded ideas—a fierce dedication to truth. Perhaps this is best summed up in the words of Charles S. Sherrington (1940, p. 400): "Truth is a 'value.' The quest itself therefore is in a measure its own satisfaction.... Our advance to knowledge is of asymptotic type... continually approaching, so continually without arrival. The satisfaction... [is] eternal."

References

Jaki, S. *The Road of Science and the Way to God.* Chicago: University of Chicago Press, 1978.
Nash, L. K. *Elements of Thermodynamics.* Reading, Mass.: Addison-Wesley, 1962.
Schneer, C. J. *The Evolution of Physical Science.* New York: Grove Press, 1960.
Sherrington, C. S. *Man on His Nature.* Cambridge, England: Cambridge University Press, 1940.

Frederick J. Dillemuth has taught general, analytical, and physical chemistry at Fordham University and at St. Peter's College, Jersey City. At present he is associate professor of chemistry at Marquette University.

When adults enter graduate programs after establishing their careers,
it is often to confront, in an interdisciplinary and deeply personal
way, questions of meaning and value.

Teaching Values for Adults: Graduate Programs in Liberal Studies

Phyllis O'Callaghan

Definitions of Values and Value Judgments

Although we all have or express values in our lives, precise meanings of the term do not exist. *Webster's New Collegiate Dictionary* (1979) gives eight meanings, but only one comes close to what is implied above, namely, the definition of a value as "something (as a principle or quality) intrinsically valuable or desirable." More to the point is the definition of "value judgment," which is described as "a judgment attributing a value (as good, evil, beautiful, or desirable) to a certain thing, action, or entity." It is important to note that this definition refers to negative as well as positive qualities, both of which are associated with values.

Whether you sided with the Argentinians or the British over the Falkland Islands crisis, whether you agreed or argued with the Republicans or the

Copies of the Constitution of the Association of Graduate Liberal Studies Programs (AGLSP) are available from Dr. Allie Frazier, P.O. Box 9651, Hollins College, Virginia 24020.

M. J. Collins (Ed.). *Teaching Values and Ethics in College.* New Directions for
Teaching and Learning, no. 13. San Francisco: Jossey-Bass, March 1983.

Democrats over the budget, whether you march in support of a nuclear weapons freeze or demonstrate against handgun control, you are expressing value judgments. Most questions of public policy, at both the national and the local level, revolve around opinions and judgments (enlightened or not) that are value-laden; that is, they express convictions about what is right and wrong, good and evil, better and worse. In the city of Washington the level of interest in and concern about such questions is intensified by the news media and by the presence of both the national government and lobbyists who are responsible for molding public opinion and channeling their constituents' interests into legislation.

Ralph Henry Gabriel (1974, p. 149), who has spent his professional life analyzing American life and thought with an emphasis on values, describes a value as "an ideal, a paradigm setting forth a desired and esteemed possible social reality." Emphasizing the positive mode, he concludes that "values are beliefs" and so "inspire members of the society to act in approved ways." Again, because values are "ideal pictures," Gabriel believes they provide "a means of judging the quality of actual behavior."

Values and Education

In a democracy, and in the United States in particular, education has been marketed as the key to unlock all doors. Thomas Jefferson believed that the future of self-government depended on the education of the populace and argued convincingly that freedom and ignorance could not prevail together. Years later, John Dewey's instrumentalist view of knowledge and education promised that education would prepare American citizens for life in a democracy. But at a time when the news media bring into the average American home images of war, murder, assassination, trials, political debates, and numerous other issues calling for judgment, many people find themselves "functionally illiterate" about their own perceptions of how things should be. We may not know how we got them, whence they came, or whether they continue to be useful or true, but values and beliefs determine the choices we make about our spouses, our friends, and our jobs, as well as our political choices. Obversely, lacking clear perceptions of what we value sets us adrift personally and socially. Our educational system often studiously avoids this area of human reflection and responsibility.

Along with (and, perhaps, related to) value neutrality is the educational trend toward specialization and professionalization. While experts are unquestionably needed in a technological society, increasingly students are pointing to a need, as one of them put it, for "purposes, goals, and reasons why we are doing what we are doing in an industrial society" since these are "becoming more confused, despite high-speed information and technology."

The words are those of a police captain, with a degree in the administration of justice, in charge of one of the most diverse and explosive precincts in the city of Washington.

A New Kind of Master's Degree

In 1974, Georgetown University joined a small band of schools experimenting with a new kind of master's degree program, one aimed at adults with professional and personal responsibilities who sought to enrich their intellectual and personal lives. Now numbering sixty-two colleges and universities, that small band extends throughout the United States and has organized itself into the Association of Graduate Liberal Studies Programs (AGLSP). Generally, these programs appeal to adults whose interests are not in specialization and technical expertise, since many already have either graduate or professional degrees. For these students, an interdisciplinary program, usually combining some required core courses with graduate liberal arts electives and the opportunity for independent study, provides the kind of flexibility and individualization seldom found in traditional master's degree programs.

What these students are looking for is accurately described by the current president of the AGLSP, Allie Frazier (1982, p. 2): "Generally, students entering GLS programs at the master's level are nontraditional in the sense that their formal education has been interrupted for varying periods of time by their entrance into careers and family responsibilities. In choosing to enter a GLS program, they seek the kind of synoptic vision that is the consequence of a cross-disciplinary approach that cuts through the arbitrary boundaries that presently limit traditional graduate education. As mature adults with a broad range of experience in the everyday world, they bring to their graduate study a heightened awareness of the limits of their college training and of the unanswered questions that confront any inquiring mind."

Besides Georgetown, some of the schools offering this kind of advanced degree in the liberal arts are Wesleyan (where it all began in 1952), Dartmouth, St. John's College in Annapolis, the Johns Hopkins University, The New School for Social Research, Hollins College, the University of Oklahoma, the University of Southern California, Southern Methodist University, and the University of Colorado at Denver. This partial list indicates the geographical and institutional variety of schools operating GLS programs.

While primarily for graduate students, Georgetown's Liberal Studies Program has a small undergraduate component as well. Currently, one hundred and forty-six degree candidates are enrolled in the program. They include Capitol Hill aides, lobbyists, military officers, teachers, physicians, lawyers, housewives, media specialists, and embassy personnel. For example, there are a pediatrician who teaches at Georgetown hospital, a homemaker with five children who is concurrently studying to be a rabbi, a landscape architect, an Army husband and wife, a school administrator and his poet wife, and two young women with diplomatic rank from the Thai embassy. For many of these students, a traditional master's degree is neither practical nor desirable. In the last fall's class, 20 percent of the students already had some kind of advanced degree.

Each graduate liberal studies program has been devised to fit the particular needs, intended audience, and strengths of the institution. All the programs recognize the need for the synoptic vision Frazier describes, which is the goal and purpose of interdisciplinary courses and which is responsive to the "heightened awareness . . . of . . . unanswered questions" that adults experience. Most of these programs have some interdisciplinary core courses. St. John's College offers a completely prescribed course of study, while Southern Methodist University requires no specific courses, although all of them are created specifically for the program. Many programs fall somewhere in between these two.

In the Liberal Studies Program at Georgetown, students take thirty hours of graduate credit, the equivalent of ten courses. Each student is required to enroll in two human values courses. These courses directly address such questions of human value as moral growth, human freedom, comparative values in major world religions, theories of justice, the nature of human purpose, and personal and professional ethical questions. Some of these are designated as core courses. They are taught by faculty members who have been with the program since its inception and introduce the student to the interdisciplinary approach and to the values synthesis indigenous to the program. At least one of the two human values courses must be a core course, and students are encouraged to take this course as early in the program as possible. Core courses change every semester. The student then selects courses from three areas of concentration: the humanities, social and public policy, and international affairs. The integrating feature is not a concentration (as the student does not have to select one), but two reflective essays, the first required one-third of the way through the program and the second required two-thirds of the way through. In these essays, students must define the theme they are pursuing as they independently, but with advice and assistance, work their way through the master's degree program. In the essays, students also describe the courses they have taken and explain how the courses are unified in a larger theme or interest. The theme may turn out to be job related, although the courses and the degree program are not so designed. For example, a student who was a colonel with the Defense Intelligence Agency noted in his reflective essay that his goal was "the formation of a critical awareness concerning the complexity of issues and the maintenance of a sound ethical framework for informed decision making." Even more specifically, a manager from the telephone company sought throughout his program to understand work-related problems of creating and establishing equal rights among those who worked for him. Another administrator, a young woman from the Kennedy Institute of Ethics, is currently choosing courses that will help her understand the limits of growth.

The last course in Georgetown's program is a seminar, during which the student, under the direction of a mentor, writes a major research paper or carries out a major project. A project could be writing a one-act play, as in the case of a teacher from a school specializing in fine arts. Recent final seminar papers have included such topics as Latin American liberation theology, substance abuse and human freedom, value conflicts as impediments to international transfers of technology, and theories of the development of the responsibility of the state. In the final seminar, students endeavor to integrate all the elements of the program. Thus, the student produces a culminating research project that usually grows out of the theme the student has established and includes some attention to questions of value.

Compared to a traditional master's degree program at Georgetown or any other university, this liberal studies degree is distinctive in that the major is not a specific liberal art, but, rather, the liberals arts at the graduate level, it is taught in an interdisciplinary mode, rather than through a single discipline, and it deals with human values, because it is based in the liberal arts. As Frazier (1982, p. 3) said, "Most courses [in graduate liberal studies] encourage our intellects and sensibilities to cut through arbitrary boundaries and to explore the values and contributions of diverse modes of knowing and seeking knowledge."

Values Orientation in the Georgetown Program

The values orientation appears in the three kinds of courses that make up the Liberal Studies Program at Georgetown. First, there are the human values core courses, which are interdisciplinary and focus on value themes. The faculty members who teach these core courses include philosophers, theologians, historians, and sociologists. These courses shift students' attention away from sterile, specialized fields of vision and toward broader, more comprehensive ones in which values implicit in the subject matter of the course are highlighted.

For example, one of the core courses is "Values in Conflict" which examines a number of areas in current social life where values actually conflict. Taught by a philosopher, one of the key areas studied is family or generational conflict. Students read Margaret Mead and Erik Erikson, as well as selections from Aristotle, Plato, and Aquinas. They also view such classic films as *Padre Padrone* and *Death of a Salesman* and discuss such plays relevant to the theme as *Oedipus Rex* and *Hamlet*.

Another core course is "Alienation and Self-Identity." Taught by a theologian, it describes the individual quest for self-identity. From an interdisciplinary perspective, the class explores the nature of the human self and its relation to society, contrasts the alienated individual with the revolutionary, and examines concepts of God and of the world as alien other in the writings of Sartre, Berger and Luckmann, Freud, Joyce, and others.

The second type of course is the human values course. While similar to the human values core course, it does not necessarily cover such broad subject matter, but it does directly confront questions of value. The course called "A World in Process," for example, deals with contemporary scientific and philosophical visions of the world and with the myths, metaphors, and paradigms whereby we consider the question of human destiny. Readings are drawn from Alfred North Whitehead, Teilhard de Chardin, and others. "Greek Ethical Thought" begins by considering early Greek views about the relationship between ethics and religion, as reflected in archaic poetry and in Aeschylus. It then moves to the writings of the Sophists and to some passages in Thucydides that document crises in Greek thought and values that occurred during the fifth century B.C. After an examination of these earlier periods, the course focuses on the new foundations for moral values established by Socrates and Plato. "Morality in Literature and the Media" builds on the life experiences of students and considers moral problems, as they appear in literature and in the media. It aims to develop moral awareness to help students make good choices. Beginning with a reading of Aristotle's *Nichomachean Ethics* and a modern companion work, Henry Veatch's *Rational Man,* the course includes discussions of a Shakespearean play, various early and contemporary works selected by students, and a current film or television program.

The third kind of course, electives created specifically for the program, is either in the humanities, social and public policy, or international affairs. While taught by professors in specific disciplines, each course must be approved by the curriculum committee of the Liberal Studies Program and must convey a sense of the interdisciplinary — the synoptic — as well as a sense of questioning. In all the courses they take, although most directly in the human values courses, students are expected to increase their awareness of the values inherent in social, economic, political, historical, and philosophical problems, issues, and situations.

An English professor, for example, teaches "Fragmentation and Reintegration," using the work of T. S. Eliot, Picasso, Sartre, Tillich, David Smith, and Henry Moore to focus on psychological, aesthetic, and moral options in our modern world of chaotic images, incoherent messages, and confusing and contradictory values. A political scientist, in his class called "The World Power Balance and Current International Issues," questions why politics are so savage and explores the nature of the nation-state system, as well as various themes of foreign policy. "Meaning in History" asks first whether human history has a meaning, a purpose outside itself or within: Is there a pattern into which the totality of events fits? Is this a subject appropriate to historians and philosophers or a genre in itself? Students then examine the answers of such thinkers as St. Augustine, Voltaire, Hegel, Vico, Marx, Spencer, and Toynbee.

As the course titles and descriptions indicate, all the courses in the Liberal Studies Program make a deliberate effort to synthesize rather than merely analyze. Focusing on specific themes, issues, questions, and problems, the courses allow and encourage students to confront perennial and current problems and recurring questions that we pose about our own identities, our past and future, unique national experiences and conflicts, international behavior, and our place in a threatened environment. Thus, the values orientation of the program is pervasive and crucial to the identity of Georgetown's program.

Graduate liberal studies programs appeal to questioning adults who like the metahistorian, Arnold Toynbee, want to weave facts into a fabric of understanding. These students are often successful professionals looking also for intellectual stimulation in a program that is academically structured, but not rigidly focused on specialized information in any one field. Another distinctive feature of the program at Georgetown is its personalization. All the students confront value questions and organize their programs around themes they construct individually. One student, for example, about to become a father for the first time, was concerned about the transmission of values from generation to generation. Another, having returned for her master's degree after twenty-six years of child-oriented activities, reflected on the degree itself as she was graduating: "It is about trying to understand the meaning in our existence and to attain whatever modicum of wisdom one's cup can hold."

In the final pages of his comprehensive review of the idea of progress, Robert Nisbet (1980, p. 332) laments the "loss of meaning or purpose," not only in America but throughout the Western world, and the accompanying "erosion of faith in Western civilization; not just political but social, cultural, and religious institutions." Many students in the program have expressed similar concerns and confusion about old, new, and changing values. A woman who is a stockbroker became interested in the program because she thought it would help her relate her work and her life to the things that were happening around her. A press aide on Capitol Hill was concerned about fundamental questions of ethics and identity. The Liberal Studies Program, he said, offered him the opportunity to pursue these questions.

The Liberal Studies Program has flourished at Georgetown not only because it meets the intellectual needs of adults, but also because the university is particularly well suited to this kind of graduate program. In March of 1981, the board of directors of the university approved a statement of main campus goals and objectives, which described liberal education and its goals at Georgetown. That statement expressed the expectation that a "liberally educated person not only seeks the true and appreciates the beautiful, but also makes the good the ultimate norm of his actions." In other words, the liberally educated person, whether a traditional undergraduate or an adult student, will find at Georgetown a concern with questions of value and will be educated as though they matter. Given the nature of the Liberal Studies Program, its requirements, and its curriculum, every Liberal Studies student should feel very much at home with this view of education.

References

Frazier, A. M. "The Concept of Graduate Liberal Studies." *The Forum for Liberal Education,* 1982, *4* (4), 2-4.
Gabriel, R. H. *American Values: Continuity and Change.* Westport, Conn.: Greenwood Press, 1974.
Nisbet, R. *History of the Idea of Progress.* New York: Basic Books, 1980.

Phyllis O'Callaghan is assistant dean of the School for Summer and Continuing Education and director of the Liberal Studies Program at Georgetown University. She recently received a grant from the National Endowment for the Humanities to conduct a summer institute in American Studies for elementary and high school teachers.

Should the teaching of ethics to undergraduates be left solely to specialists in ethics, or does the very nature of the task require a cross-disciplinary effort?

Who Should Teach Ethics?

Carol J. Rizzuti

In these times of specializations and subspecializations, the question of who should teach ethics to undergraduates — even if posed by a philosopher — seems readily answerable. Is it not axiomatic that a subject should be taught by the person who is most qualified to teach it, that is, by a specialist in that subject? It would seem that, just as a college expects its English department to take full responsibility for the teaching of Chaucer, it should expect its philosophy department to take full responsibility for the teaching of ethics. But philosophy as a discipline thrives on paradoxes, and the paradox here is that, while philosophers are likely to be among the best trained in formal ethics, the subject cannot be taught successfully if it is taught only in philosophy classes.

Why should this paradoxical situation arise? What makes it inappropriate to relegate the teaching of ethics to the specialists? The answer, I think, lies partly in the goals we seek to achieve in teaching ethics, and, more fundamentally, in the nature of the subject matter itself.

The Goals of Teaching Ethics

Examining the goals of teaching ethics is not an easy task. In the first place, the field of ethics is usually divided into three related but distinct inquiries. Even if we consider only general introductory-level undergraduate courses in ethics, the goals of those courses will depend partly on the particular

M. J. Collins (Ed.). *Teaching Values and Ethics in College.* New Directions for Teaching and Learning, no. 13. San Francisco: Jossey-Bass, March 1983.

ethical inquiries that are being pursued. There is, first, the giving of an objective, descriptive account of the ethical behavior and standards of various people—descriptive ethics. Then, there is the analysis of the meaning, justification, and status of ethical terms and theories—metaethics. Finally, there is the determination of what things are good and bad, right and wrong, obligatory and nonobligatory, and of the reasons that can be given for these judgments—normative ethics.

Even within a single dimension of ethical investigation, particularly within normative ethics and metaethics, there is considerable disagreement over what should be taught. There is no one system of conduct accepted by all nor one way of analyzing ethical terms nor one set of criteria in terms of which different ethical positions can be evaluated. There is even disagreement over whether ethics can and should be taught at all: Are there any objective ethical realities, or does reality consist only of what can be measured, quantified, observed, and duplicated? If there is a real ethical dimension to life, can knowledge of it be taught? ("Can virtue be taught?" queried Socrates.) And if we think that ethical realities exist and that ethics can be taught, does that mean ethics should be taught? Is there a way to teach ethics without indoctrination? In other words, can ethics be taught without violating the very conditions on which ethical imperatives exist—personal responsibility and personal freedom?

These are extremely important and difficult questions, questions that require continued serious investigation. For the purposes of this chapter, though, I shall assume some basic answers. First, the kinds of ethics courses I shall consider here are those general introductions to ethics that, in varying proportions, take a normative and metaethical approach. Second, I shall start from the premise that there are ethical realities, and that there is at least enough agreement about these realities to allow discussion to begin. I shall assume further that it is possible to teach ethics—in fact, obligatory to do so— without using methods of indoctrination. I shall work from the premise that the teaching of ethics to undergraduates is something we want to do.

What is there, then, about the goals of teaching ethics that makes it unlikely for us to achieve these goals solely with courses on ethics? Daniel Callahan (1980, pp. 64-69) suggests five goals, which he believes are applicable to all ethics courses: "stimulating the moral imagination," "recognizing ethical issues," "developing analytical skills," "tolerating—and reducing— disagreement and ambiguity," and "eliciting a sense of moral obligation." The first four goals are, I believe, similar to the goals we would set for most undergraduate courses in the liberal arts and the sciences. For "stimulating the moral imagination," we might substitute "stimulating the aesthetic imagination" or "stimulating scientific curiosity and imagination." And we would certainly want students of any subject to be able to recognize the issues involved in the subject and to develop the requisite skills to deal with them. The goal of learning to tolerate disagreement is, perhaps, more uniquely required in the teaching of ethics, where, as Callahan points out, the very nature and existence of morality is brought into question. I believe, though, that even here good analogies can be found in the methodological disputes and opposing viewpoints of other disciplines and in the ways these disciplines deal with their internal conflicts.

Callahan's last goal — eliciting a sense of moral obligation — hints at the essential difference between ethics courses and other undergraduate courses. It is this goal that implies most clearly a concern with the future moral behavior of the students who take courses on ethics. It can be shown that reference to behavior is an essential element not only in the goals of ethics courses but also in explaining why the teaching of ethics cannot be relegated solely to courses on ethics.

Let us explore further just what we want an ethics course to do. If our aims were simply to introduce students to the methods of ethical analysis and ethical argumentation and make them more sensitive to the ethical dimension of life and more tolerant of different viewpoints, then there would be no reason to assume that these goals could not be fully accomplished within an ethics course, just as we assume that analogous goals can be accomplished within other undergraduate courses. The measure of an ethics professor's success in achieving the aims of the course would be the students' performance on exams, presentations, and papers. Thus, the teaching of ethics would be fundamentally akin to the teaching of other academic subjects.

Even a cursory reflection on these goals, however, shows that they do not adequately express what we actually want an ethics course to do. One of the central principles of morality is that ethical concerns pervade life and must never be ignored. If this is so, then the goals involved in teaching the content matter of ethics (considered as an academic discipline) must carry with them an additional goal: that students who take an ethics course continue throughout their lives to use what they have learned. If, as teachers, we believe ethical imperatives are pervasive and paramount in life, then it would be inconsistent for us to remain indifferent to the ethical problem of whether our courses will help or hinder students in their efforts to develop morally.

Ethics Courses Are Rightfully Concerned with Students' Behavior

This is not to say that a course on ethics should seek to change students' behavior; attempting to do so would violate not only the requirements of ethical teaching but also the free will and personal responsibility necessary for ethical action in the first place. Callahan (pp. 69–70) forcefully argues that changing students' behavior is not a goal appropriate to an ethics course. He points out (p. 70) that "it is not change per se that should be the goal, but the potentiality for change as a result of ethical analysis and judgment." What we want an ethics course to do is help students acquire the skills they will need to recognize and make moral decisions and help them see the importance of acting in ways they have judged to be moral. It is in this important sense that an ethics course is rightfully concerned with students' behavior.

It may be objected here, though, that it is not only ethics professors who are in some way concerned with the effect of their courses on the behavior of their students. Is it not one of the goals of an art course, for example, that students gain from it an appreciation of art, as well as a capability and willingness to enjoy future aesthetic experiences? Is this goal not similar to the goal of making students appreciate the importance of ethical concerns and willing to take account of ethical imperatives if they are confronted with ethical situations in life? Actually, these two goals are not alike. In the case of other courses, the aim of fostering an appreciation of the subject and a willingness to pursue the subject after the course had ended is a desirable but not a necessary goal. In the case of ethics, however, this goal is both desirable and necessary.

If a student completes an art course and never again has occasion to confront a work of art, we may well believe that the quality of the student's life has been thereby diminished, but we can still reasonably say the student has learned the subject, and we can still reasonably believe that the student will be both capable of and willing to use that knowledge should the occasion arise. Similar arguments could be made for the other disciplines. We might very well be willing to say that a student had learned literature in an English course, even though that student never read another literary work after leaving the course, or that a student had learned physics in a physics course, even though he or she never had the occasion to use that knowledge in life. As with the art example, the quality of the student's life might be judged to be thereby impoverished, and we might wonder whether the student had truly learned to appreciate the value of literature or the value of physics, but there is still a meaningful sense in which we could say that he or she had learned literature or learned physics. There is also a meaningful way in which we could test this: by having the student take an exam comparable to the one previously passed in the physics course or the English course.

With respect to ethics, however, it makes no sense to speak of someone who has taken an ethics course and learned the subject matter of the course, as measured by the usual testing procedures, but who has never had occasion to use in life what was learned in the course, even though he or she would be willing to do so should the opportunity arise. The reason this makes no sense is that ethical problems are pervasive in life, and if a person claimed not to have confronted these problems while still professing a genuine willingness to do so, we would say either that the person had not learned what an ethical situation is or that the person had learned once but had then forgotten. The ability to do well on an ethics test would be irrelevant here. If such a person did do well, we would, I suspect, attempt to find some explanation for his or her incongruous success (such as that he or she had guessed at the answers). Even if we could find no such explanation, we would be unwilling to say that such a person had learned ethics; to have learned ethics, one must have recognized the pervasiveness and unavoidability of ethical imperatives in life. Unlike the situation with other academic subjects, the possibility of a person's having ethical knowledge, but no occasion or requirement to use it, is ruled out. Consequently, our goal that students continue to use what they have been taught becomes, in an ethics course, not only desirable but also necessary.

It may be possible, of course, to learn ethics and then be unwilling to use what has been learned — the classical problem of weakness of will. Even if this is possible (and there is a serious question as to whether one can truly know what is right and not do it), the very existence of the problem of knowing what is right but doing what is wrong points to the intimate connection we perceive to exist between ethical knowledge and ethical action.

We should note, further, that the failure to act in an ethical way does not necessarily implicate a course on ethics, even if one has been taken. Similarly, high moral behavior cannot be automatically attributed to a college course on ethics. There are many influences other than ethics courses on how one behaves. What interest us here are the goals of ethics courses and the question of whether concern with students' moral behavior is a special and necessary element of these goals, and we have seen that it is.

The Relationship of Ethics to Other Courses

Granted, though, that when we teach ethics we must (at least to some degree) be concerned with the effect of the course on our students' behavior — more precisely, with their potential to behave in ways they judge to be moral — why does this mean that the teaching of ethics must not be left solely to the specialists on ethics? Surely we can think of other kinds of courses aimed even more directly at affecting behavior but that are taught best by specialists. Consider the courses offered in medical schools and law schools. These courses often aim directly at the future actions of the students who take them, yet we would think it inappropriate for them to be taught by anyone other than physicians or lawyers. Why should this not also be true with respect to the teaching of ethics?

There are some significant differences between undergraduate ethics courses and courses offered in professional schools, differences that make the effect on students' behavior far more difficult to control in courses on ethics.

First, students who take courses in professional schools take them, for the most part, to learn how to be good practitioners of their chosen professions. This may or may not be the case with college courses in ethics. Some students do take them because they are sensitive to ethical issues and want to increase their abilities to deal with them. Others take them because they are required courses or because they are offered at convenient times or with popular professors or because of various other considerations that may be extraneous to the goal of learning ethics. The willingness to learn and change, which can usually be assumed of those taking professional school courses, cannot be so readily assumed of undergraduates taking ethics.

Second, there are strong positive reinforcements for professionals to use the skills they have been taught, and few pressures against their doing so. The same does not hold true for ethical actions. What morality requires is often extremely difficult and in opposition to worldly rewards.

Third, the standards by which performance is judged are far less clear in ethics than they are, for example, in medicine or in law. While neither medicine nor law is an exact discipline, there are still fairly well agreed-upon standards for evaluating the performance of a physician or a lawyer, and teaching these standards is not particularly problematic. This is not true for ethics; the criteria by which we judge ethical behavior are themselves a subject of debate. Moreover, both the ethical requirement that people take responsibility for their actions as well as the multiplicity and richness of ethical situations pose special difficulties for the teaching or formulation of such criteria.

Fourth, students learn how to practice a profession primarily from the courses and training they take at a professional school. Ethical principles are learned in the classroom, at home, from friends, from religious institutions, and from a variety of other sources. Consequently, there are many forces that rightfully compete with what is taught in the course. Thus, these four differences between ethics courses and the kinds of courses taught in professional schools are sufficient to invalidate the argument that because the latter can be taught adequately by specialists alone, the former can as well.

We have seen that there is a special and necessary connection between the teaching of ethics and the concern for the future moral behavior of those who have been taught. We have seen that ethical imperatives are pervasive and demand, by their very nature, to be taken seriously at all times. We have also seen that, as a result of numerous factors, teaching ethics and succeeding at the goal of helping students develop morally is an exceedingly difficult task.

For all these reasons, ethics cannot be taught in ethics courses alone. If we are truly required to act morally, this requirement binds us in all areas of our lives. Teaching ethics only in courses on ethics fails to take account of this requirement and conveys implicitly the idea that one can be a mathematician, for example, and, as such, not have to deal with ethical questions, or that one can become adept at literary analysis without ever having to make an ethical decision while performing such analysis. If this were the case, we might wonder whether an ethical person could rightfully devote his or her life to the study of mathematics or literature. In fact, though, viewing other academic disciplines as basically amoral endeavors contradicts the ethical claim that ethical questions arise in all areas of our lives. If one accepts this claim, then failing to include ethical discussions in the teaching of other subjects is a failure to teach those subjects adequately. If this ethical claim is correct, then there is in fact an ethical dimension to those other subjects, whether or not this dimension is explicitly presented. Just as ethics cannot be fully taught if it is relegated to ethics classes alone, neither can other subjects be fully taught without any reference to ethical questions. The relationship is reciprocal.

This is not to say that professors of other disciplines must repeat in their classes what can be presented more properly in courses on ethics. Ethical questions are nevertheless involved in other disciplines, and full presentation of other disciplines requires such questions to be addressed. Moreover, if we take seriously the ethical mandate to act ethically in all areas of our lives, then we must at least be prepared to show our students how this mandate can be carried out within the other academic areas they study. Part of what we mean when we praise a person as having acquired a liberal education is that he or she is able and willing to make value judgments and to differentiate between ethical and nonethical responses to the world.

Earlier educators had, perhaps, a clearer perception than we do of the centrality of ethical issues. As Douglas Sloan points out (1980, p. 2), the course in moral philosophy was once considered to be the "capstone" and unifying force of the college curriculum. We have moved away from this early concept of education and now give recognition to the contributions of specialists. Specialization, however, cannot be allowed to restrict the teaching of ethics, a subject which by its very nature defies specialization. If we wish to educate our students, we must make them aware of the ethical dimension of life, and since the ethical dimension pervades all of life, each discipline, in its own way, must contribute to the achievement of this goal.

References

Callahan, D. "Goals in the Teaching of Ethics." In D. Callahan and S. Bok (Eds.), *Ethics Teaching in Higher Education.* New York: Plenum, 1980.

Sloan, D. "The Teaching of Ethics in the American Undergraduate Curriculum, 1876–1976." In D. Callahan and S. Bok (Eds.), *Ethics Teaching in Higher Education.* New York: Plenum, 1980.

Carol J. Rizzuti is an assistant dean at Fordham College of Fordham University and an adjunct assistant professor of philosophy. She received her doctorate from the Johns Hopkins University. Her dissertation was in the philosophy of religion.

Teaching ethics in a communications program
primarily involves the imparting of method.

Locating Ethics in Mediaworld

John M. Phelan

There are two kinds of students in most graduate communications programs: those who plan to make a career in one of the communications professions, which embrace a broad collectivity from journalism to film production; and those who wish to study communications as researchers, writers, and analysts of the social significance and philosophical relevance of the communications professions. In educating these two different kinds of students, the approach and the goal are somewhat different. As the man to blame for graduate communications studies (and, particularly, for teaching ethics at my institution), I must be sensitive to this difference as well as aware of the fundamental unity between understanding and action. Let me discuss students oriented toward a professional working career first, and then those who wish to pursue a life of the mind in the context of communications research.

Case Scenarios and Conscience Sensitivity Training

All of ethics is involved in all of life. Consequently, it is naive to believe that there is a special ethics for people in specific vocations. Rather, the evolved routines of the professions and the social settings established around these routines create a context within which human decisions are either made or evaded. Preparing people for a profession surely involves opening their eyes to the reality, and not the romantic stereotype, of the human structure within which they will be called upon to make decisions that have moral consequences.

M. J. Collins (Ed.). *Teaching Values and Ethics in College.* New Directions for Teaching and Learning, no. 13. San Francisco: Jossey-Bass, March 1983.

The common way of going about this task is to use what I call the "special case" scenario, which is particularly prevalent in journalism programs. Here, one plunges into notorious controversy, takes no side, and presents the "dilemma" that editors, reporters, press secretaries, and others must "face": Should a travel writer accept a luxurious junket from an airline? Is it proper to give money to a news source or a famous figure in order to have exclusive publication rights? Should newspaper owners dictate editorial policy to their professional employees? Should a reporter reveal the identity of a news source to a grand jury in a criminal investigation? Should foreign correspondents or international scholars bend to CIA pressure to use their positions as cover for some secret mission?

The general public is familiar with these types of publicized cases and with many others. In the classroom, the special case scenario tends to degenerate into a "laundry list" without any overarching intellectual rubric of principle, while principles are what ethics is all about. The special case scenario also tends to confine moral responsibility within dramatic stereotypes, draining everyday professional life of its moral dimension. Finally, from an ethical point of view, most of these cases are not very special at all: They involve honesty, loyalty, integrity, and justice in applications that are considerably less subtle than those in biology, say, or in married life.

I recall a pleasant, martini lunch with a highly placed network official. Politely curious about my work in communications ethics, he offered, without obvious irony, "Gee, I don't think I have ever run across an ethical problem after twenty years in the business." If we as educators do our jobs better, we may hope that our students will not be so blessed.

If the special case scenario is not too effective, what else can we do? Consciousness raising, in reverse. By that, I do not mean sleep induction, but a reverse of Paulo Freire's original purpose, which was to make the poor and the exploited of Brazil (and elsewhere) understand exactly why and how they found themselves in their position, with the hope that such awareness would get them out of that condition through consequent action. What we try to do is *conscience sensitivity training* — that is, getting the aspiring professional to realize that actions result from free decisions, and that he or she is thus reponsible for the consequences of those decisions.

Conscience sensitivity training operates at two levels. The first level involves honest self-assessment. The second level involves scrupulous awareness of the particular world in which one has chosen to live and operate. At the first level, there are very few real moral dilemmas for most people. Honest self-assessment is a matter of motivation, not of knowledge. The question is rarely "What am I to do?" It is more often "Do I have the courage to do what I know to be right, just, loyal, truthful, or (at a very advanced level) self-sacrificing?" Extreme or borderline cases make interesting dramas that illuminate subtleties, but most of us do not encounter subtleties. I have learned that when I say to myself, "It is all so complicated," I am in fact trying to make it easy. Moral imperatives are clear, but often they are painful and discomfiting to obey. At this level, then, conscience sensitivity training is aimed at getting people to acknowledge the irritating relevance of an ethical ideal to a pedestrian and even humdrum situation, when they would rather pretend that everything is automatic and preordained. "If I don't do it, somebody else will" — this useful evasion is equally applicable to shoplifting and contract murder. So many communications professionals never make decisions; they obey the automatic dictates of the marketplace, because the "real world" has a "bottom line."

This brings us to the second level of conscience sensitivity training. What, indeed, is the real world? Most crime in the twentieth century has been justified in the name of some necessity that "forced" people to act in a way they would have avoided if they had not had to live in the real world. Whatever it is, the real world is, alas, very much of our own making.

Elsewhere (Phelan, 1977), I have called the world my students will live in "Mediaworld." What is Mediaworld like? We can describe it in terms of its peculiar language and of its characteristic work procedures. For many years, J. R. R. Tolkien worked on the invention and development of a new language with its own alphabet, syntax, and grammar. As a gifted etymologist, Tolkien eventually was able to fabricate all these characteristics, but was chagrined to learn that he still did not have a language. A language must flow from and reflect back to a culture, a tradition, a history, and above all, a mythology. Therefore, Tolkien created a mythology and became world-renowned for *Lord of the Rings*. The defect Tolkien corrected is, in contrast, a desired goal in Mediaworld linguistics. Mediaworld's language must drain its vocabulary of the blood of history, tradition, and mythology. Its messages must be cut loose from all connotative ties to culture — and, therefore, to moral, humane consciousness. It is a language analogous to the ingenious "signalgrams" for luggage, toilets, handicapped-reserved areas, and dining facilities that we associate with international airports and their concourses of strangers who are presumed to have no shared heritage. DeWitt Wallace saw the great distribution value of such a language and pioneered it at *Reader's Digest* which significantly has a number of foreign language editions and an immense circulation. The language is so precedent-free, assumption-low, and contextless that one can read most *Digest* non-narrative articles in any order; the paragraphs are interchangeable. This kind of language is the stuff of most advertisements, commercials, and radio and television news. A good example of its extreme form can be found in civil defense manuals, which say things like: "In the event of an atomic attack, you may experience radiation sickness. High fever often accompanies radiation sickness. For fever, take aspirin and plenty of liquids."

True; but certainly not the truth. I call this type of language the "paragram." Paragramming is most appropriate in the *Digest* and in owner's manuals for Japanese appliances, where it is sorely missed. But to paragram questions of war and peace, sexuality and loyalty, commitment and community is to evade such questions.

Paragramming ignores moral questions to the point of extinction, and the marketing pressures that encourage writers to paragram editorials, political speeches, medical and insurance advertisements, governmental policy reports, and virtually every other public discourse of Mediaworld are creating an amoral world. This is, perhaps, a major reason why so many people believe that they have never run into a moral or ethical problem. There is no place for such problems in their language and, thus, in their consciousness; therefore, they are finally without conscience, what C. S. Lewis (1947) called "men without chests."

Mediaworld is secondly characterized as the final stage of depersonalizing (and, therefore, demoralizing) industrialization. Craftsmen of the past may have done careful or shoddy work, but they were personally identified with it; it was their handiwork, in the literal sense. The assembly line did away with this sense of identification with the work and has given rise to wry warnings not to buy a car made on Friday. Anyone who has ever had to get automotive repairs knows how everyone distances himself from the work and refuses to take responsibility for it. Mediaworld has introduced the assembly line to the world of human intercourse. Telephones are answered by machines with prerecorded messages that are written by a paragrammer, read by a professional actress, and contain policy decisions made by faceless committees. Who is saying what to whom? If a network anchorman were to give out false information, no one would hold him responsible; he might apologize for the news division and retract the statement, but more than likely, the false report without legal threats from aggrieved parties, would be let through the stream, and a later "update" would give "more recent developments." Paragram in, paragram out, paragram forever. It was this context which permitted Ron Ziegler (Nixon's quondam press secretary) to face provable accusations that he had knowingly lied with the explanation he "misspoke" himself. A glitch in the system, not a morally reprehensible act, because an act outside the context of moral awareness.

Mediaworld, then, is the workplace of communications professionals and, in many ways, is also the world we all live in, dependent as we are on the media for our information, entertainment, and (in some measure) our politicians. It is instructive to consider how this industrialization of consciousness has changed the parameters of moral awareness. Let us take the example of persuasion and propaganda: There is nothing immoral about persuasion; it is what makes the world go round, from young men wooing young ladies to the

Sermon on the Mount. But there is a feeling that the amorphous set of activities labeled *propaganda* is contemptible and dangerous. What is the difference?

Politics and married life are both made up of leaders and led, of compromises, of deals. Ultimately, some courses of action will prevail over others. Life consists of getting people to do things. A fairly consistent body of moral development considers brute force, or "might makes right," an immoral way of getting things done. We are left with talking people into things. We can do this quite directly ("Call an ambulance!"), but this approach is usually limited to obvious necessities. More usually, indirection is called for ("So you are an Aquarius. Say, wouldn't you like to. . ."). The entire panoply of techniques that have not progressed much beyond Aristotle can be employed—flattery, fear, guilt, merit by association, and so forth. What all these methods have in common is that they involve interchanges among alleged equals who know the rules of the game—with an advantage to the one more linguistically skilled and more astute at the psychological assessment of others. Persuasion is an art, a craft identified with the persuader. When the persuader is separated from his argument and he or she is a mere talking "gun for hire," we sense that something unethical may be involved, as the Ancients did with the advent of the Sophists. Above all, persuasion is an intensely and, perhaps, even disagreeably personal transaction.

Modern times have brought great influxes of strangers from the familiar countryside to the impersonal city. The machine that brought them together also could help control them; the age of mass persuasion was born, the age of so-called engineered consent. In this period, there has been a belief that control of the media, a monopoly of channels of information, meant control of the masses. Goebbels, Churchill, Franklin Delano Roosevelt, Fidel Castro, John F. Kennedy—each of these very different men living in different societies shared this conviction and acted on it, with varying success. Aristotle's art of persuasion was updated to a "science" using the latest technologies of presentation on the sending end and of reaction measurement on the receiving end. The art of persuasion, it was believed, was being replaced by the science of propaganda—or, to paragram it, the "science of public education."

The unrest of the 1960s disproved the effectiveness of these mechanical methods all over the world, from the cultural revolution in China to the "greening" of America. Mediaworld has now evolved beyond propaganda to something called *attention management.*

In the Second World War, American strategists at first planned to plod through the Pacific island by island, beach by bloody beach, on the way to Japan and ultimate victory. Fortunately, this laborious mistake was scrapped in favor of "leapfrogging." A few strategically located islands could be taken, and the rest could be isolated and ignored. The technicians of propaganda, such a distance from the craftsmen of rhetorical persuasion, realized that it was not so easy to change people's minds, but that it did not matter so much. The ultimate goal of the persuader is to change behavior, and persuaders had always naively presumed that you had to change people inside before you could change them outside; minds and hearts must be won. Vietnam made the concept of "winning minds and hearts" a painful memory. But, can you change behavior *without* changing minds? You bet: Cultivate a semi-stupor in your audience, and then manage what little attention is left. Get that half-attention focused on some simple bit of behavior, and then drill, drill, drill. All you have to get people to do is pull a can off a shelf or pull a lever in a voting booth — leapfrog the brain. The technique is quite sophisticated, but it can be flagged by the growing use of background music for almost all commerical messages, spoken as well as sung, for mutual fund investing as well as hair-spray. I believe we are even close to having newscasts with theme music, for similar marketing reasons — "Hail to the Chief" for presidential news; a return to the early newsreels, but with a very different purpose. Focusing on behavior rather than on motivation means totally ignoring morality and leveling all activity to equal meaninglessness. Cornflakes and candidates are chosen with equal attention and inattention and with equal sense of responsibility. From rhetoric to persuasion to propaganda to attention management to behavior modification to automatism.

I believe that sensitizing students to these issues is what ethical education is all about. The honest, imaginative reportage of models like James Fallows, Frances Fitzgerald, Taylor Branch, and many others who write with a moral perspective proves that rejection of Mediaworld is growing among younger people. It is our task to guide and shape this rebellion by tying it in with the great moral traditions of the past.

Ethics and Communications Research

Communications research is an area even broader than the active pro-fessions. At one extreme, it is exotically scientific, as in the dazzlingly abstruse mathematics of information theory, which Bell Telephone has put to such amazing use for increasing its efficiency. In this area, communications research really is a branch of engineering and physics. At another extreme, we have the critical studies of people from the Frankfurt School: Jürgen Habermas, Leo Lowenthal, and Theodor W. Adorno, for example. Quite evidently, ethical values are prominent in this latter group (whether or not they are applied as we would wish) and remote or implicit in the former, where they are more associated with ultimate use, rather than with methodological assumptions. Ethics is relevant to all communications research, but in different ways, depending on the type of research.

Twenty odd years ago, Marshall McLuhan wrote the last of his seriously intended works and aptly titled it *Understanding Media*. One did not have to agree with McLuhan that his way was the only way to understand media or even that it was a correct way, but one did have to acknowledge, however, that he tried to explain a collection of disparate phenomena from a unitary perspective with explicit assumptions. At that time, the beginning of the Age of Aquarius, the media hype that surrounded McLuhan was making him into something of a circus guru, a market strategy that he somewhat shabbily collaborated in and that enraged serious scholars like Dwight Macdonald. But compared to the pop sociology and adolescent tracts *about* the media that are touted today *by* the media, McLuhanism appears, on reflection, something like Unitarianism. Whether or not he succeeded, whether or not he was well-mannered and decorous, McLuhan belonged to a tradition of scholarship in which the words *argument* and *treatise* referred to definite methods of pursuing a craft. In his own quirky way, McLuhan was trying to do something comparable to what Darwin did with fossils and turtles—fit his meticulous observations of particulars into an organizing vision that located the yet-to-be-observed on some sort of graspable continuum.

At the present time, when Delphi studies are classified as "research" and undisciplined jeremiads are called "theses," it behooves any graduate program to inculcate certain standards and a respect for method as ethical ideals. Research is a way of life with noble traditions; it is not a license to erect prejudices into principles. This much is fundamental. Once this idea is established (and it never should be taken for granted), we can begin to criticize the studiously amoral standards of so-called functional research—the intellectual parent of market research and public opinion surveys, whose purpose is to facilitate commercial or political strategies, rather than to explain a part of the real world.

Thus, there are two ethical concerns involved in teaching communications research to students. The first is the ethical ideal of truthfulness and integrity of method; this concern looks to the value *of* the research. The second is an examination of the purpose of (and assumptions about the real world involved in) the type of research pursued—the values *in* the research. The second concern is more important, more subtle, and more obviously related to the teaching of ethics, but the first is an ineluctable presupposition of the second, without which we have empty pieties delivered from a podium. The teaching of ethics, then, in a communications program involves primarily the imparting of method. How are we to work? How are we to think about what we are doing? How are we to evaluate the world in which we will be working? Above all, how can we change the common expectations of our world to favor the good over the expeditious?

References

Adorno, T. W. "Culture Industry Reconsidered." *New German Critique,* 1975, p. 6.

Freire, P. *Pedagogy of the Oppressed.* New York: Herder and Herder, 1970.

Habermas, J. *Communication and the Evolution of Society.* London: Heinemann Educational Books, 1979.

Lewis, C. S. *The Abolition of Man.* New York: Macmillan, 1947.

Lowenthal, L. *Literature, Popular Culture, and Society.* Palo Alto, Calif.: Pacific Books, 1967.

Macdonald, D. "Incomplete Nonsense: The McLuhan Massage." In *Discriminations: Essays and Afterthoughts 1938–1974.* New York: Grossman, 1974.

McLuhan, M. *Understanding Media.* New York: McGraw-Hill, 1964.

Phelan, J. M. *Mediaworld: Programming the Public.* New York: Continuum, 1977.

Suggestions for Reading

Brown, L. *The Business Behind the Box.* New York: Harcourt Brace Jovanovich, 1971.

Diamond, E. *The Tin Kazoo.* Cambridge, Mass.: MIT Press, 1975.

Epstein, E. J. *News from Nowhere.* New York: Random House, 1973.

Phelan, J. M. *Disenchantment: Meaning and Morality in the Media.* New York: Hastings House Publishers, 1980.

Real, M. *Mass-Mediated Culture.* Englewood Cliffs, N.J.: Prentice-Hall, 1977.

Schudson, M. *Discovering the News.* New York: Basic Books, 1978.

Steiner, G. *In Bluebeard's Castle.* New Haven: Yale University Press, 1971.

John M. Phelan is professor of communications and director of graduate communications studies and of the Center for Policy Studies in Ethics and Communications at Fordham University in New York. In the spring of 1982, the Fordham Center presented a symposium on international communications control with the participation of the United Nations, UNESCO, Reuters, the Associated Press, VISNEWS, Argus Newspapers of South Africa, the Caribbean News Service, Interpress, and Interlink. In addition to his own books and articles, Professor Phelan has edited research project reports for the Institute of Social Research.

What happens when an ex-POW of Hanoi determines
to teach a course in moral philosophy?

The Stockdale Course

Joseph Gerard Brennan

When Commander James Bond Stockdale lay in prison in North Vietnam, he
told himself that if he ever got out alive he would teach a course in moral philosophy. After seven and a half years in captivity, much of that time in solitary
confinement and under torture, he was released at last and returned to the
United States. Promoted rapidly to vice-admiral and appointed president of
the Naval War College at Newport, Rhode Island, he introduced and taught
just such a course. I helped him organize the course and served as his tutor
and team-teacher, staying on to teach the course at the War College after
Stockdale retired from the Navy in 1979. The course is still going strong and
draws full enrollment from the military officers who make up the student body
of the Naval War College.

Because of its association with the ancient philosopher Epictetus, the
name Stockdale caught my attention in a brief news item from *The New York
Times* in the fall of 1975:

Rear Admiral James B. Stockdale, who was a prisoner of war in North
Vietnam for seven and a half years, has been presented with eight medals for,
among other things, "resisting all attempts by the North Vietnamese to use
him. . . ." In 1973, after his release, Admiral Stockdale wrote of his experience,
"When I ejected from that airplane in 1965, I left my world of technology and
entered the world of Epictetus. I was alone and crippled; self-reliance was the
basis for daily life."

M. J. Collins (Ed.). *Teaching Values and Ethics in College.* New Directions for
Teaching and Learning, no. 13. San Francisco: Jossey-Bass, March 1983.

The original source of Stockdale's remark about the contrasting worlds of technology and Epictetus was a column written by Stockdale, then still a Navy captain, that appeared in *The New York Times* of Sunday, April 1, 1973. I had missed seeing that piece, which caused little reaction outside military circles at the time.

Admiral Stockdale and Epictetus

Curious as to what this man had found in the old Stoic philosopher to sustain him in his long ordeal, I wrote to him. Almost by return of post, I received a lengthy reply. I give it here in full because it affords necessary insights into the character of Admiral Stockdale and reveals his motive for establishing the course that was to bear the title "Foundations of Moral Obligation."

> I was honored to receive your inquiry about the comfort and strength philosophical readings gave me throughout my seven and a half years in prison. Perhaps I can best explain how this came to be with a rather rambling chronology.
>
> I came into the Navy as a Naval Academy midshipman in 1943 at the age of nineteen. For the next twenty years or so I was a rather technically oriented person. I was a seagoing destroyer officer, an aviator, a landing-signal officer, a test pilot and academic instructor at the test pilot school, a many-times-deployed fighter pilot, and ultimately, a squadron commander of a supersonic F-8 Crusader outfit.
>
> In 1960 I was sent to Stanford University for two full years of study in politics, history, economics, and so on, in preparation for later assignments in politico-military policy making. I loved the subject matter, but noticed that in many courses my interest would peak at about the time the professor would say, "We're getting into philosophy — let's get back to the subject." I had more than adequate time to get the expected master's degree and suggested to my adviser in my second year that I sign up for some courses over in the philosophy corner of the quadrangle. He was dead set against it — thought it would be a waste of time. He said, "That's a very technical subject — it would take two terms to learn their peculiar vocabulary." Finally, after I persisted, he said, "It's up to you."
>
> It was my good fortune on that first morning that I wandered through the halls of the philosophy department, grey-haired and in civilian clothes (or course), to come by an open office whose occupant looked me in the eye and asked if he could be of help. When I told him that I was a graduate student in the humanities with no formal philosophy background, he could scarcely believe it. When I told him I was a

naval officer he asked me to have a seat. He had been in the Navy in World War II. His name was Phillip Rhinelander. To jump ahead, his background was as follows: As a Harvard lawyer, he had practiced in Boston for fifteen or twenty years before Pearl Harbor, volunteered for war service at sea, and thereafter took his Ph.D. at Harvard under Whitehead. After tours as a dean at Harvard and Stanford, he was back in the classroom, at his own request. He was in the midst of his two-term "personal" course: "The Problems of Good and Evil." This he had built upon the lessons of the book of Job ("Life is not fair"). He offered to let me enter the course and, to overcome my shortcomings of background, to give me an hour of private tutoring each week. What a departure from the other departments! (In some, Ph.D. candidates sat outside their adviser's office for hours on end, awaiting a ten-minute conversation.) I loved Rhinelander's class, and particularly our hour together each week. I remember how patient he was in trying to get me to realize the full implications of Hume's *Dialogues on Natural Religion* (I still have page after page of notes on that).

To jump ahead again, I completed the course in fair fashion, and went on to others from a visiting professor from Michigan named Moravcsik, but Epictetus had already come into play during my last tutorial session with Rhinelander.

As we parted after our last session, he reached up to his bookshelf and said something like, "As I remember it, you are a military man — take this booklet as a memento of our hours together. It provides moral philosophy applicable to your profession." It was *The Enchiridion.*

That night I started to peruse my gift. I recognized nothing that applied to the career I had known. I was a fighter pilot, an organizer, a motivator of young aviators, a martini drinker, a golf player, a technologist — and this ancient rag talked about not concerning oneself with matters over which one had no control, and so forth. I thought to myself, "Poor old Rhinelander — he's just too far gone." Nevertheless, I read and remembered almost all of it, if for no other reason than that it was given to me by the man I had come to worship as the most complete human being I had ever met — a sensitive scholar, a man who devoted himself to teaching quality kids quality concepts after a full career of legal and academic administrative success, a music composer, a kingpin of all major phases of university life, and a sophisticated gentleman of kindness and generosity.

About three years after I had said goodbye to "poor old Rhinelander," while in the midst of my second combat tour against North Vietnam as a wing commander, I pulled off a target one September morning in the midst of heavy flak, when all the lights come on (fire warning, hydraulic failure, electrical failure, and so on). As I sped over the treetops, it became immediately apparent that I had lost my flight controls—by reflex action I pulled the curtain and ejected—and was almost immediately suspended in air 200 feet above a village street, in total silence except for rifle shots and the whir of bullets past my ear. So help me, in those fleeting seconds before I landed among the waiting crowd, I had two vivid thoughts: (1) Five years to wait (I had studied enough modern Far East history and talked to enough forward air controllers in the south to fully appreciate the dilemma of Vietnam—I turned out to be an optimist by two and a half years). (2) I am leaving that technological world and entering the world of Epictetus.

The world view of the stoics, Professor Rhinelander had joked, was that their environment was a buzz saw, in which human will was the only salvation. I was to spend over four years combatting a veritable buzz saw (until the torture and extortion machine was set in idle in the late autumn of 1969) and over three more years of simple deprived detention of the sort one would expect in a primitive, hostile country. Over four years were to be spent in solitary confinement, nearly half of it in leg irons. Throughout, until 1970, every effort was to be made to break my will, to make me a cat's paw in tinhorn propaganda schemes. Real or fabricated "violations of the established regulations for criminal's detention" (for example, tapping on the walls to another prisoner) would result in torture, with the end aim of sequential confession of guilt, begging for forgiveness, apology, and atonement (signing an antiwar statement). A similar sequence would be set up with particular gusto if I were found to be exercising leadership of others via the tap code ("inciting other criminals to oppose the camp authority").

The situation was thus framed in the above context. I was crippled (knee broken, eventually to become rigidly fused by nature; shoulder broken, partial use of arm), alone, sick (weight down by fifty pounds), depressed (not so much from anticipating the next pain as from the prospect of my eventually losing my honor and self-respect), and helpless except for will. What conditions could be more appropriate for Epictetus' admonitions? As a soldier, I had bound myself to a military ethic:

Chapter XVII of *The Enchiridion*

Remember that you are an actor in a drama of such sort as the author chooses—if short, then in a short one; if long, then in a long one. If it be his pleasure that you should enact a poor man, see that you act it well; or a cripple, or a ruler, or a private citizen. For this is your business — to act well the given part; but to choose it belongs to another.

I was crippled:

Chapter IX of *The Enchiridion*
Sickness is an impediment to the body, but not to the will unless itself pleases. Lameness is an impediment to the leg, but not to the will; and say this to yourself with regard to everything that happens. For you will find it to be an impediment to something else, but not truly to yourself.

I was dependent on my extortionists for life support and soon learned to ask for nothing, to avoid demands for "reciprocity":

Chapter XIV of *The Enchiridion*
Whoever then would be free, let him wish nothing, let him decline nothing, which depends on others; else he must necessarily be a slave.

I could stop my misery at any time by becoming a puppet. Was it worth the shame?

Chapter XXVIII of *The Enchiridion*
If a person had delivered up your body to some passerby, you would certainly be angry. And do you feel no shame in delivering up your own mind to any reviler, to be disconcerted and confounded?

Relief from boils, heat, cold, broken bones was available for the asking — for a price. What should I say?

Chapter XXIV of *The Enchiridion*
If I can get them with the preservation of my honor and fidelity and self-respect, show me the way and I will get them; but if you require me to lose my own proper good, that you may gain what is no good, consider how unreasonable and foolish you are.

Epictetus was not the only valuable philosophic memory in my predicament: Job ("Why me?... Why *not* me?"), Descartes' bifurcation of mind and body, and many other readings were invaluable.

It is important to note that I am speaking only for myself. Some of my prisonmates had more doctrinaire religious concepts, which served them well; some drew resolve from their concepts of political virtue, and so on, in a broad spectrum of varying levels of sophistication. Thoughts of God and country helped me, too — but my "secret weapon" was the security I felt in anchoring my resolve to those selected portions of philosophic thought that emphasized human dignity and self-respect. Epictetus certainly taught that.

This has been a much longer explanation than I had planned, but I am enthusiastic about the wonders a man in your profession and discipline can bring about in the lives of people in need. I wish I had the qualification to be in your shoes, teaching in a good school. From firsthand experience, I am committed to the position that the study of moral philosophy is a particularly relevant part of education. And though education, as one of my favorite quotations reads, may be but an ornament in prosperity, it is a refuge in adversity.

Moral Philosophy at the Naval War College

More correspondence followed. In late 1977, Stockdale asked me to come up to visit him at the War College in Newport. In a sunlit office overlooking Narragansett Bay, I found myself stared at by a man who looked a little like James Cagney in his prime, but more handsome. Piercing blue eyes bored into me from under a shock of thick, prematurely white hair. Stockdale wore the blue- and white-starred ribbon of the Congressional Medal of Honor on his uniform. Intense, feisty, and impatient with anything but directness, Stockdale moved about restlessly, stumping back and forth on his leg that had been broken by the fall from his plane and rebroken by beatings from his captors. He asked me if I would help him put together a course in moral philosophy and team-teach it with him. I had just retired as professor emeritus of philosophy at Barnard College of Columbia University and was on the point of accepting a State Department offer of a Fulbright lectureship in India. Stockdale said, "Phone those characters in Washington and tell them to go to hell." I did so, politely, and we set to work at once on organizing the course.

The Naval War College, I found, offered a one-year graduate course of study to military officers in midcareer. The curriculum centered on three core courses — strategy and policy, defense economics and management, and naval operations. Upon assuming the War College presidency, Stockdale had expanded the elective course offerings to twenty or thirty, the number depending on the particular trimester in which they were offered. All the elective courses, except the new offering in moral philosophy, were related in some way to the three required core courses. The student body at the Naval War College consisted of about 300 midgrade military officers ranging in age from thirty-two to forty-two and in rank from lieutenant commander to commander, or major to lieutenant colonel. There were a few Navy and Coast Guard captains, as well as a handful of colonels from the other services. About half the student body was in the Navy, with the rest split among the other services. A very few civilian officers from various government agencies were also enrolled. Two small groups of foreign officers formed autonomous but integrated colleges within the larger whole — the Naval Command College (senior) and the Naval Staff College (junior). All the officers wore civilian clothes, as did the military faculty, except on days when high-ranking Pentagon officers made official visits.

How were we to organize the Stockdale course for this formidable student audience? The first question was the title. Stockdale did not much like the word "ethics." He thought the comtemporary "ethics explosion" had eroded the older, nobler sense of the word. He knew that ethics courses were spreading rapidly, not only in military institutions, but also in business, industry, and the professions. Harvard Business School had become ethics-conscious, IBM and Electronic Data Systems Corporation were working on ethics, and the Cummins Engine Company had taken on a professor of ethics from a major university. Stockdale was uneasy about this trend. He did not want his course to be the military equivalent of what he called "Ethics for Dentists." He preferred the term "moral philosophy" to "ethics"; the former seemed to suggest the tradition of the humanities, and he believed that, without some background in the humanities and some familiarity with the ancient and modern philosophical classics, it would be hard to teach ethics without boring students, at the very least. Stockdale was convinced that semieducated people (and, in his opinion, that group included many academics) tended to reduce ethics to a branch of psychology. Training in the humanities, Stockdale believed, would show that much of what goes by the name "social science" serves up ideas expressed earlier and better in classical philosophy and modern literature.

Stockdale was convinced, too, that a course in moral philosophy for military officers did not need to be organized directly around military ideas or writings on military ethics. The study of good philosophy and literature, he held, would benefit human beings; and, since military officers were human, it would be good for them, too, not only as human beings but also as military officers.

"Foundations of Moral Obligation"

"Foundations of Moral Obligation" was the title we finally agreed on. We had only a ten week trimester to get through the course's readings, lectures, lectures, seminar discussions, papers, and examinations. The course opened with the idea of the Hermetic — the alchemical transformation that may occur when a human being is subjected to intense pressure within a crucible of suffering or confinement. Stockdale's own *Atlantic Monthly* article "The World of Epictetus" (April, 1978), led easily to discussions of the prison experiences and reflections of Socrates, Boethius, Cervantes, Wittgenstein, Sartre, and Anwar

Sadat. We went on to readings and discussions of the book of Job, the Socratic dialogues of Plato, Aristotle's *Nichomachean Ethics,* Kant's *Foundations of the Principles of the Metaphysics of Morals,* and Mill's *On Liberty* and *Utilitarianism.* These readings were supplemented by selections from the works of Emerson, Sartre, Camus, Conrad, Koestler, Dostoyevsky, and Solzhenitsyn. The course closed, completing a circle, with a reading of Epictetus's *Enchiridion,* the little book which Phillip Rhinelander had given to Stockdale and which sustained him in prison — a Stoic work Albert Salomon describes as "a manual for combat officers."

Reflecting on the course years later, Stockdale (1982) said, "We studied moral philosophy by looking at models of human beings under pressure, their portraits drawn from the best materials we could find in philosophy and literature. The professional implications for military men and women followed. We did not have to draw diagrams; the military applications came up naturally in seminar discussions" (p. 98). Recently, Stockdale came across a monograph called *The Teaching of Ethics in the Military,* published by the Hastings Institute (Stomberg and Wakin, 1982), an ethics think-tank. He exploded at this sentence: "A flight leader threatens American values if he cannot analyze a moral problem." In his review of the monograph, Stockdale (1982) wrote, "That's not helpful. A flight leader threatens *human* values — and, by inclusion, American values — if he hasn't the guts ('character') to act like a man" (p. 98).

Stockdale believed that, before one can teach moral philosophy, one must decide whether to emphasize rules or character: both are necessary, of course. As senior officer of the Hanoi "Alcatraz," Stockdale exacted obedience to a stern set of rules. "Our value systems [in Alcatraz] had in common, " he wrote in "Back from Hanoi" (*The New York Times,* April 1, 1973), "the fact that they were based on rules, that they placed unity above self and that they precluded self-indulgence." But, for Stockdale, rules were always secondary to character in considerations of moral life. He agreed with Aristotle that the end of a man is to be as human as possible. To achieve this fulfillment is an art that can be learned only by hard habit and stressful training. Acting well and living well follow from character, from what a man is. While he found Sartre's dictum "A man is the sum of his acts" challenging, Stockdale still held that to do something one must be something. He was less enthusiastic about Aristotle's heavy emphasis on the primacy of reason in the moral life. To our class that first year at the War College, he quoted Dostoyevsky's underground man: "You see, gentlemen, reason is an excellent thing, there's no disputing that, but reason is nothing but reason and satisfies only the rational side of man's nature, while will is a manifestation of the whole life, that is, of the whole human life, including reason and all the impulses."

Stockdale liked the way that, for all their differences, both Dostoyevsky and Aristotle supported the reality of individual freedom and personal responsibility. He endorsed Dostoyevsky's rejection of the Socratic axiom that humans act only in accord with what they think is good for them. He had seen men knowingly choose the bad and consciously rush head down to their own destruction. Like the underground man, Stockdale declined any social system that made men into "piano keys" and believed that any society scientifically organized according to the principles of rational self-interest would end, at best, as a harmonious anthill.

Among Stockdale's favorite pages of Aristotle's *Nichomachean Ethics* were those in which the philosopher distinguishes between voluntary and involuntary action, analyzes the role of choice and intention in human acts, and describes the way free choice and compulsion can coexist. Stockdale denied the existence of brainwashing; one was always responsible. If one broke under torture—and everyone did, at some point—one could always make the torturers start all over again the next day. His captors did not like to do that, Stockdale remarked; it made things so much easier for both sides if the victim "cooperated." When his comrades, racked by twisted ropes, had "spilled their guts" and returned to their cells weeping from shame, Stockdale would comfort them via the tap code on the wall: "We've all done it. Just make them work for it. Don't give anything away free." And so, to our Naval War College class, he read from the *Nichomachean Ethics:* "There are some instances in which such actions elicit forgiveness rather than praise, for example, when a man acts improperly under a strain greater than human nature can bear, and which no one could endure. Yet there are, perhaps, also acts which no man can possibly be compelled to do, but rather than do them he should accept the most terrible sufferings and death." Stockdale himself had risked death when he beat himself into bleeding insensibility with a wooden stool to prevent himself from being filmed for North Vietnamese propaganda purposes.

Student Reaction to Stockdale's Course

The Naval War College has a detailed course evaluation system, and the student-officers are frank in their estimates. How did they react to the Stockdale course? Most of them admired Stockdale just short of idolatry and gave the course very high ratings. A few found the admiral ill at ease in the more intimate seminar discussion sessions. All applauded the chance the course had given them to read the works that were discussed. For the greater part of their military careers, these military officers had concentrated on highly technological material. The writings and thoughts of Aristotle, Kant, Sartre, and the others were mostly a new experience for them, but they were quickly at home with these writers. Woody Hayes came one day to visit the class and was delighted to hear that Wittgenstein's *Was kommt leicht hat keine Wert* was no more than his own charge to his old Ohio State football teams: "If it comes easy, it ain't worth a damn."

The first midterm examination was formidable; Stockdale and I were determined (it was a mistake, of course) to throw everything in. Senator John Glenn was visiting that day, and Stockdale brought his old classmate to my office. Clutching a copy of the midterm Stockdale had proudly thrust upon him, John Glenn stood shaking his head in bewilderment, saying, "Pretty heavy test, Professor!" Meanwhile, screams of anguish from officers taking the test down the hall were painfully audible.

What the officers liked best of all about the Stockdale course was the opportunity to reflect on questions they felt had always been in their own minds, but just below the surface. This course, they agreed, provided them their first chance to raise those questions to the level of mature consciousness. At the close of the school day, the car pools back to the officers' homes and families at Fort Adams and Coddington Cove resounded with arguments on what they had heard that day, what they had read the night before, and how they saw it in the context of their own lives and work. A conversation repeated to me disclosed that one carpooler had said, "Kant's ethics is all right in theory, but in practice, it won't work," to which his comrade had replied, "But Kant's not telling how people do act or what does work, but how they ought to act and what should work." That officer had done his homework for the course.

During the year we taught together, I passed on to Stockdale a number of passages from my own reading. These he carefully copied onto his note cards, of which he kept a voluminous file. One of his favorites was a remark Sartre made in 1940 to a Catholic priest, when both were prisoners of war in a German camp at Trier. In his *Avec Sartre au Stalag 12D,* Fr. Marius Perrin recalls the remark "L'Important n'est pas ce quon a fait de vous, mais ce que vous faites de ce quon a fait de vous"—"The important thing is not what they've made of you, but what you make of what they've made of you." Stockdale had good reason to endorse that belief; he had lived it.

Reading List

These were the reading assignments for "Foundations of Moral Obligation." This list, except for minor revisions, is the same one offered when the Stockdale-Brennan team taught the course for the first time in the fall of 1978.

Week One *From 20th Century Technology to the World of Epictetus. The Meaning of Moral Philosophy.*

Stockdale, J. B. "The World of Epictetus." *Atlantic Monthly,* April, 1978.

Koestler, A. *Darkness at Noon.*

Gabriel, R. A. "The Nature of Military Ethics."

Walzer, M. "Prisoners of War."

Week Two *The Book of Job. Life Is Not Fair. The Problem of Evil.*

"The Book of Job." *Old Testament.*

Solzhenitsyn, A. *One Day in the Life of Ivan Denisovich.*

Week Three Socrates. *Doctrine and Example. Civil Disobedience. Can Virtue be Taught? Soul and Body.*

Plato, *Euthyphro, Apology, Crito,* and *Phaedo.*

Week Four Aristotle. *Happiness as Living Well and Faring Well. The Moral and Intellectual Virtues. Courage as Balance and Endurance.*

Aristotle. *Nichomachean Ethics.*

Conrad, J. *Typhoon.*

Week Five Kant and Hart. *Ethics of Moral Duty and Civic Law. Motives and Consequences. "Ought" and "Right." The Meaning of Natural Law.*

Kant, I. *Foundations of the Metaphysics of Morals.*

Hart, H. L. A. *The Concept of Law,* Chapters Eight and Nine.

Week Six Mill. *Morality as Social Utility. Justice and the Greatest Happiness Principle.*

Mill, J. S. *Utilitarianism* and *On Liberty.*

Dostoyevsky, F. *Notes from the Underground,* Part I.

Week Seven Individualism and the Collective, I.

Emerson, R. W. "Self-Reliance."

Sartre, J. P. "Existentialism Is a Humanism."

Camus, A. *The Plague.*

Week Eight Individualism and the Collective, II.

Marx, K., and Engels, F. *The Communist Manifesto.*

Lenin, V. I. *What Is to Be Done?*

Dostoyevsky, F. "The Grand Inquisitor" from *The Brothers Karamazov.*

Week Nine Science and Values. *Does the Universe Have Meaning or Purpose?*

Monod, J. *Chance and Necessity.*

Smith, H. *Kamongo.*

Week Ten Return to the Beginning. *Epictetus. The Stoic Ideal and the Ethics of the Military Officer. Philosophy as Technical Analysis and Way of Life. Wittgenstein and the Ethics of Silence.*

Epictetus. *The Enchiridion.*

Wittgenstein, L. *Tractatus* (selections)

Malcolm, N. *Ludwig Wittgenstein: A Memoir*

Plato. *Phaedo* (rereading of opening and death scene)

Stockdale, J. B. "Freedom." *Parade,* June 29, 1980.

References

Stockdale, J. B. Untitled review of *The Teaching of Ethics in the Military. Naval War College Review,* 1982, *35* (5), 97–99.

Stomberg, P. L., and Wakin, M. *The Teaching of Ethics in the Military.* Hastings, N.Y.: The Hastings Institute, 1982.

Joseph Gerard Brennan, professor emeritus of philosophy at Barnard College of Columbia University, is now electives professor and academic adviser to the Naval Command College, Naval War College, Newport, Rhode Island. He is the author of six books and various articles on philosophy and on comparative literature. His recent essay, "Alfred North Whitehead: Plato's Lost Dialogue," appears in Masters: Portraits of Great Teachers *(Joseph Epstein [Ed.]. New York: Basic Books, 1981).*

Admiral James Bond Stockdale is now senior research fellow at the Hoover Institution, Stanford University, where he is writing a book about his experiences as a Navy flier and prisoner of war.

Since the student affairs office deals with students in the complexity of their lives outside the classroom, it is and should be actively and centrally involved in values education.

The Role of Student Affairs in Values Education

William R. Stott, Jr.

It seems to me that any discussion of the role of the student affairs office in values education has to establish at the outset that the student affairs office is first and foremost part of the university's teaching mission. This point must be emphasized and inform the everyday operations of all its departments if the student affairs office is to play any role at all in the teaching of values. If the student affairs office does not take this active pedagogical role, then it really has little or no significant place in the university. The locution "student services," often applied to an office of student affairs, suggests a certain passivity on the part of the staff and an elective aimlessness on the part of the students, qualities that diminish the active educational impact a good office of student affairs should have.

It follows, then, that a student affairs division will best realize its contribution if its programs are consistent with the educational mission of its university. Since any effective student affairs division is unique to the institution of which it is a part, the details of this discussion derive inevitably from a particular university. At the same time, however, the proper goals of a student affairs division, as I conceive of them, are shared by student affairs personnel at many different institutions. These are to enrich, extend, and amplify the goals of a particular university and to create a context that not only allows

M. J. Collins (Ed.). *Teaching Values and Ethics in College.* New Directions for Teaching and Learning, no. 13. San Francisco: Jossey-Bass, March 1983.

education to take place but also actively teaches. My own experience at Georgetown University provides the context of this discussion.

Educating the Whole Person

My interest in the student affairs office derives from my experience as a teacher. I think anyone who teaches in a classroom soon recognizes that much of the learning process occurs outside, in an environment that may or may not support what goes on in the classroom. The teacher also soon discovers that the whole learning process is enormously complex and endlessly fascinating and works in a variety of ways. There is an old axiom that one can teach either by precept or by example. As we get involved with the learning process outside the formal and often artificial confines of the classroom, we inevitably become involved with the multi-faceted possibilities of the learning process, with affective as well as cognitive learning. It is a privilege and an opportunity to become involved in the totality of students' lives. Much catalogue rhetoric and educational literature have been devoted to the ideal of educating the whole person. While we always fall short of this expressed ideal, at Georgetown it is always taken seriously, partly because it is completely consistent with the 400 year-old Jesuit ideal of education.

When we talk about the education of the whole person, we mean the education of the person's mind, body, and spirit. I believe that, except in the realm of abstraction, it is impossible to talk about these elements separately; they all are interdependent and mutually reinforcing. By becoming involved in educating the whole person, we find the best way to address the potential inherent in values education, for it is precisely by addressing the whole functioning person that we come in contact with that person making choices and acting in the world, and these choices and actions have value. Furthermore, emphasis on teaching the whole person makes a teacher less and less capable of ignoring the manifold responsibilities that are part of such a commitment.

One of my principal concerns about our fulfilling our function as teachers is the smothering and overwhelming role of specialization in higher education. I do not, like some "Miniver Cheevy," long for a world without specialization; we have come too far for that: Specialization is necessary and has an enormous potential for good, and it helps little to whine about it. I do contend, however, that specialization informed by the goals of a value-laden liberal arts education will be a richer specialization, supported by a sense of context and therefore accountable for its actions. In our increasingly complex world, we often rest content with or take refuge in the accomplishment of the narrower goals of specialization. It is bad enough that this is often true in matters of curriculum, but it is worse yet when we see the curriculum as something unrelated to those areas of student life that are the responsibility of the student affairs office.

Because of the real and justifiable demands for competence in any specialty, it becomes harder and harder, in both curricular and co-curricular matters, to establish the ground for a true liberal arts education that will facilitate the integrative process and help students make the good normative. Georgetown students, for example, are bright, ambitious, and energetic. They tend often to look through the undergraduate experience toward professional school or some career. They are "pre-med", "pre-dent", "pre-law" and often define themselves by their majors. In addition to the fact that such definitions are sadly reductive of the richness of their individuality, such self-designation provides a self-fulfilling prophecy of narrowness: Students do not stop to take advantage of the great riches available to them.

The student affairs office can work against that kind of narrow intellectual or spiritual tunnel vision and provide a context in which broader-based learning that involves both self-discovery and involvement with others can occur. Student affairs personnel continually have to examine, in concert with faculty and deans, the philosophy and purposes of their institution — those things, in short, that make the school unique. It follows that student affairs programming should be at least as well thought out as the curriculum is. Indeed, it should not be victimized by the departmental approach, as curriculum making can be. I believe, for example, that the student activities program or the athletic program should not merely represent a passive response to the expressed needs and desires of the student body at any given time. These programs should, rather, represent an educational statement that reflects the ideals and goals of the university. The student affairs staff should be fully involved in examining and reflecting on these ideals and goals, both as they are explicitly set forth and as they are embodied in the culture and traditions of the institution.

Values Implications of Student Affairs Work

The importance of student affairs personnel in values education cannot be overemphasized; the staff must be aware of and sensitive to the moral implications of the learning experience. These individuals, after all, are often the front-line teaching representatives of the university's philosophy of education. They are present in situations where students are confronted with the need to make serious decisions about sexual conduct, drug use, relationships with others, and crises of belief and commitment. All these things are undeniably part of the learning process. The realities of the examined life and the search for the true and the good occur largely outside the classroom.

Student affairs personnel, therefore, are often the principal representatives of perceptible standards, for students see student affairs personnel in the daily conduct of their lives more than they see many faculty members. In a sense, student affairs personnel are subject to scrutiny on the part of the student body that other faculty members are not, because our specialized method of education, wherein responsibilities of the faculty are to a department and a discipline, makes it difficult for faculty members to spend much time with students outside the classroom.

If our commitment to an integrated values education is to be realized, it is extremely important that students be exposed as much as possible to the adults who represent that commitment. Here, student affairs personnel can fulfill a major teaching role in the university in at least two ways: They can serve as examples of adults who are attempting to lead integrated, thoughtful, compassionate lives; and despite the very real difficulties of doing so, they can develop ways of including the faculty in the kind of active interplay with students through which the faculty can bear witness to principles enunciated in the classroom and, thus, teach by example.

Some years ago I sent a letter to the faculty at Georgetown asking for volunteers to go into residence halls and talk with students informally about vocational or other interests. Over 150 faculty members responded, and the office of student affairs was able to publish a book listing the faculty volunteers and the topics each one had volunteered to discuss. Over the years, our office has made possible many such informal but value-laden meetings, which have been very helpful in breaking down artificial barriers between the faculty, the administration, and students.

In addition, we have tried, whenever possible, to get the faculty involved in committees and discussions to maintain dialogue between the faculty and the student affairs office. A number of us in the student affairs office at Georgetown also have faculty appointments and teach formally. What is most important, however, is that members of the student affairs staff know from the beginning that they are regarded as teachers and that their role is to be fulfilled with that principle in mind. When one perceives oneself as working at being a teacher, one is inevitably conditioned by that perspective and sets priorities accurately. This perception is contagious, too, and, in large measure, conditions the entire climate in which a student affairs staff works.

Specific Positions and Programs

The drive for specialization and the narrowness it encourages create a need for positions or programs that can move in the direction of wholeness, breadth, and integration. Several years ago I founded two positions that specifically address some of the imperatives of a values education. The first was that of the district action coordinator, whose initial charge was to inventory and assess the value of the existing social programs at Georgetown. I wanted to support and enrich the programs that seemed particularly effective and consistent with the University's ideals and goals and eliminate the others. Although there are, of course, people involved in these programs who are not Christian, the orientation of this program was, and is, unabashedly Christian. The educational purpose of the district action program is to provide students an opportunity to apply in the community some of what they have studied and discussed in the classroom. In fact, in some cases, we have fourth credit options or practicums for selected courses in theology and economics, for example.

This year a group of students and faculty are discussing, more specifically, faith and justice issues and the ways they are and should be reflected in the curriculum. All this is also consistent with our desire to try to impart the idea that an education is a distinct privilege which imposes upon the privileged a grave responsibility for others. I think the program has been a success. We now have over 500 undergraduates involved in a whole host of social programs, which include soup kitchens, helping the aged, tutoring children, and addressing housing problems in the inner city. These programs have been a very effective way of exposing people to some of the larger problems of human existence, and they also work against what can be a selfish specialization.

The second position I founded was that of coordinator of the arts, whose job was to do for the arts the same things the district action coordinator was to do for our social programs. This position was created with the conviction that the arts are by definition integrative and synthesizing and correct the kinds of reductive specialization that work against the aims of the liberal arts. The fact that the arts speak of the beauty and coherence of a realized ideal is again consistent with the tradition of Georgetown University.

Georgetown is predominantly a residential university, and, to some degree, we can coordinate our residence-hall programming with the ideals that inform the university, creating a context where living and learning are mutually supportive and understood to be related. We have a special-interest housing program, in which students with a common interest live together in an environment organized to support that interest. The arts hall, for example, is a dormitory where students who have an expressed interest in the arts live together and, by virtue of this expressed interest, tend to reinforce one another and amplify their opportunities both for performing and responding to performances by others. Another special-interest corridor is organized around the principle of social service. Students living in this group form a kind of activist core for many of our social action programs.

Three years ago cooperation between the office of student affairs and the college of arts and sciences led to a grant from the American Association of Colleges, Project Quill. This grant began an experiment called, for lack of a better term, "the living-learning floor." All the freshmen residents of one dormitory floor take at least two courses in common each semester. They are selected from among required courses in philosophy, theology, and English. The faculty members teaching these courses often share cocurricular activities and meals with the students. Upperclassmen residents of the hall share an inter-disciplinary seminar that addresses such topics as world hunger. The experiment was so successful that, after the grant ended, the students came to the residence hall staff and asked that the project be continued. Those of us involved were happy to continue it. In teaching my poetry course in this program, I find that our formal classroom interaction is much more richly informed because of activities and discussions we share outside the classroom. Faculty members and students interact in a better way because, knowing one another better, we get involved in discussions about educational and career choices in the context of the students' whole lives. Inevitably in such a personal environment, questions of value are central to such discussions.

Georgetown's distinct religious character has given it another important kind of living-learning environment. This year, for example, we have twenty-five religious, twenty of whom are Jesuits, living in our residence halls and acting as corridor ministers. Their presence is positive and supportive. They are neither disciplinarians nor hall monitors, but they give special meaning to the residential experience by being available. It is also important to note that the presence of an active campus ministry team, with representatives from a number of denominations, provides numerous liturgical and counseling opportunities. Obviously, an active team can be significant in providing those occasions of reflection, contemplation, and discussion that are so essential to values education.

We have found that the roles of the student health service, the counseling center, and the center of career planning and placement can also be enormously supportive of the university's mission, as it relates to values education. This is so because the staffs of these departments see themselves as actively teaching and therefore significant to the university's principal mission. Some of the best counseling with regard to education as a process, for example, occurs in the counseling center. Specific problems of growth and development are addressed, and these problems always involve values choices. Students must see that their education is part of this process and that their satisfaction with themselves and their ability or inability to get along with others are parts of their education—that there is a marriage, or should be, between what happens in the classroom and what goes on outside. Coping with a personal problem or making a career decision should both be informed by a sense of values; nothing is done in isolation. Questions of value are, finally, utilitarian.

The Integrative Ideal

The wide range of concerns falling within the province of the student affairs office makes it almost inevitable for student affairs personnel to interact with students in many ways important to shaping their values. A mistaken perception of the student affairs office separates its activities from students' academic learning, yet student affairs activities often reach students at points of greatest concern and intensity. An honestly conducted athletic program, for example, recognizes that our physical nature is fundamental to a fulfilled humanity. The principles of fair play, honesty, discipline, and effort, which are developed particularly in team sports, make an obvious contribution to values education.

In their characteristic fragmentation of educational subject matter into individual courses within specialized departments, the academic programs of most universities have lost touch with the integrative ideal of education. Faculty members may even acknowledge how much learning takes place outside the classroom, but still find themselves confined to classroom teaching. A thoughtful and effective office of student affairs whose programs reflect the goals and ideals of its university can make a major contribution to teaching and learning by meeting students on their own ground and helping them integrate their formal learning with the variety of experiences, both good and bad, that they will have in college.

Perhaps a homely analogy will be helpful. When we meet bright, articulate, thoughtful young men and women in our work, they generally come from bright, articulate, thoughtful homes. While it may not seem so on many campuses today, I still think that — in a way which is elaborate, sophisticated, and not easy to define — the university represents for its students a bright, articulate, thoughtful home. Most of the learning that occurs in any home is the product of example, not of precept. The university, then, represents a commitment to the belief that learning and education require unified teaching on the part of the whole institution. The thing that precisely distinguishes a fine university from a mediocre one is a greater proportion of intelligent, caring adults. That kind of personalism, informed by a generous sense of something outside oneself, makes a great institution.

William R. Stott, Jr., is vice president for student affairs and dean of students at Georgetown University. He regularly teaches a course in poetry for undergraduates and a course in Shakespeare for graduate students in the Liberal Studies Program.

The editor concludes the sourcebook and offers
some suggestions for further reading.

Conclusion and Additional Sources

Michael J. Collins

I would like to conclude this volume with a story about a good friend of mine.
His name is Richard Kershaw. When Richard graduated in 1963 from Car-
dinal Hayes High School in the Bronx, he knew he never wanted to go to
school again. He joined the Air Force, served in Italy and Taiwan, toured
Europe and the Far East, and was discharged four years later.

His first job after leaving the Air Force was repossessing cars. His territory was the South Bronx. You know what the job entails. If you were to buy a
car on credit and not keep up the payments, Richard would arrive in your
neighborhood at about three or four o'clock in the morning and steal the car
back for the credit company. (I leave it to you to imagine what might happen if
you were caught stealing somebody's car in the middle of the night in the
South Bronx). It is not the kind of job you would want to keep for the rest of
your life.

Richard's next job, with the same company, was what is called a credit
man. A credit man's job is to approve or disapprove loan applications—in this
case, for new car sales. Richard told me that, in comparison to being a credit
man, repossessing cars was pure joy. The credit man, in the auto industry at
any rate, has an impossible job: He is caught in the middle—between the car
dealer, who wants the loan approved so that he can sell the car, and the credit
company which wants to avoid loaning money to people who will not repay it.
In one ear you have the dealer: "Look, if I don't sell this car, I'll lose my fran-

M. J. Collins (Ed.). *Teaching Values and Ethics in College.* New Directions for
Teaching and Learning, no. 13. San Francisco: Jossey-Bass, March 1983.

chise." In the other ear you have the company: "Look, if we don't get our money back, you are responsible." It is not the kind of job you would want to keep for the rest of your life. I tell you these things about Richard because I want you to know that he did difficult, frustrating, sometimes dangerous jobs in a demanding, competitive, high-pressure industry.

When I first met Richard, he had changed his mind about college and was a student in the School of General Studies, Fordham University's evening college for adults on the Rose Hill campus in the Bronx. He was going to school at night, majoring in English, and working as a credit man. Two years later, he graduated first in his class with a 3.9 index, spent a week in law school before deciding the law was not for him, and then went out to look for a new job.

Like many other people who change jobs, Richard ended up at an employment agency. He filled out the forms and was called in. (If you've ever been in the situation, you know the indignities you endure.) In the course of their conversation, the interviewer asked him, "What was your major, Richard?" (They always call you by your first name.) "English," he said. "You know, Richard," said the interviewer, "it's a tough world out here, and we don't have much time to lie around reading books." This was the interviewer's response to someone who had spent six years in a pressure cooker — repossessing cars, making difficult decisions with a phone in each ear, and at the same time earning a degree *summa cum laude*. Richard resisted the desire to repossess the interviewer's teeth and walked out of the office.

The story has a happy ending. Today, Richard has an important and responsible job and he is, by the world's measure, a successful man. But if you asked him, he would tell you that it is not the job and the good salary that make him successful. What make him successful, he'd say, is that he has managed, despite all the demands and pressures of a career, to remain intellectually alive and curious; to understand, in some ways, at least, the people with whom he lives and works; to make some sense of his life and to find some answers to those nagging questions about the meaning of things. And if you pressed him, as I have, to tell you why he has been able to do these things, he would give you the answer he didn't give that silly interviewer: "It was the books I read at Fordham — not just in literature, but in philosophy, theology, history, the social sciences, and all the rest. The courses I took, the books I read, the thinking I did, and the papers I wrote not only gave me the skills I need to do my job, but also offered me a chance to give some attention to my life and to figure out what is important and what is not. I've been, I think, a very lucky man."

I conclude with this story because it is true and because I think it suggests what, at their best, teaching and learning are all about.

Additional Sources

Since the contributors to this sourcebook have been especially generous in their suggestions for additional reading, I shall list here only a few titles that may be helpful.

The Carnegie Quarterly (Spring/Summer 1980, *28,* [2 and 3], 1–7) on "Applied Ethics: A Strategy for Fostering Professional Responsibility," provides a good review of the work of the Institute of Society, Ethics, and the Life Sciences in Hastings-on-Hudson, New York—better known as the Hastings Center—since its founding in 1969. It also gives a list of the nine monographs published by the center on the teaching of ethics in higher education. (For further information contact Daniel Callahan, Director, Institute of Society, Ethics, and the Life Sciences, 360 Broadway, Hastings-on-Hudson, New York 10706.)

Derek Bok, the president of Harvard University, discusses the social responsibilities of the university in an important book called *Beyond the Ivory Tower* (Cambridge, Massachusetts: Harvard University Press, 1982). "Universities," he says at one point, "must constantly address moral issues and ethical responsibilities in all their relations with the outside world."

Kenneth Eble's *The Craft of Teaching* (San Francisco: Jossey-Bass, 1978) is a wise and honest book that has a great deal to say about values and teaching, for it continually reminds teachers that the perfection of their craft involves the generous, loving service of other human beings.

John Granrose's *Perspective on Ethics* (Athens: The Georgia Center for Continuing Education) is a videocassette eight-part series and study guide exploring how modern man makes ethical decisions. U-matic ¾″ videocassettes are available for rent or purchase as well as study guides from the Georgia Center.

Timothy S. Healy, S. J., the president of Georgetown University, has published an essay called "Belief and Teaching" (*Daedalus,* 1981, *110,* 163–175), in which he asks "What educational difference does it make if a school or college begins with and continues to hold a belief in God?"

Arthur Levine's book *When Dreams and Heroes Died* (San Francisco: Jossey-Bass, 1981) offers, as its subtitle puts it, "a portrait of today's college student." Levine points out in his preface that "The level of altruism among current undergraduates is low. It has been replaced by an ethic of 'looking out for number one' and an almost single-minded concern with material success."

Richard L. Morrill's *Teaching Values in College* (San Francisco: Jossey-Bass, 1980) analyzes the ways in which values are taught in colleges and then offers its own comprehensive program of values education. The book also contains an annotated bibliography of current literature and a lengthy list of references.

Robert J. Roth, S.J., has written an essay on the development of the Values Program at Fordham College. Called "Moral Education at the College Level: A Blueprint," it is included in a book edited by Thomas C. Hennessy, S.J., *Values/Moral Education: The Schools and the Teachers* (New York: Paulist Press, 1979). Fordham's careful experiment in values education may prove helpful to educators at other colleges and universities as they grapple with the question of values and teaching.

Michael J. Collins is dean of the School for Summer and Continuing Education at Georgetown University. He was formerly associate dean of Fordham College and director of its Values Program.

Index